The Oral literature of the Guarasug'we

An extinct horticultural people of eastern Bolivia

By

Robert Nickol M.A.

Table of Contents

Introduction 1

Cantos in mythic time 29

Cantos of spirits and souls in the present time 85

Cantos of the ways of humans and animals 111

Cantos influenced by Christianity 150

Cantos of the recent past 154

Works Cited 163

Introduction

The importance of Guarasug'we literature

The literature of the Guarasug'we is important, for it clearly has intellectual merit. This collection of stories is an exploration into another world. The stories are explorations into the frames of mind of a people unlike ourselves. This collection of stories is an exploration into another world. The stories offer us an opportunity to look at cultural patterns that perhaps could be added to our own culture.

An examination of the culture of the Guarasug'we offers us a strong, clear cultural contrast to our own culture, for these people lived apart in remote areas far away from global culture, and they retained a cultural purity. They lived in an independent sustainable culture. Although many Guarani cultures adapted to global change, the Guarasug'we did not. The rejection of Christianity by the Guarasug'we did not protect or secure their future, and the concept that Christianity is the bane of native culture is very doubtful.

Although clearly traditional and not a radical departure from the whole of Guarasug'we culture, these stories are the extraordinary expressions of a gifted story teller. The story teller is a man named Tesere, and he is the author of the majority of the stories contained in this volume. Tesere provides us with an intimately detailed look into the culture of the Guarasug'we. His eloquence profoundly expresses the anguish of a dying culture.

These stories offer us an opportunity to look into the processes of cultural death. How the global economy pursues and destroys whatever stands in its path.

Cultures have disappeared throughout history. Attempts to preserve them are faced with the problem of linguistic change or babel. For example, these stories were translated into Spanish by Tesere et al. And then they were translated into German by Dr. Riester, and then they were reformed by a professional translator back into Spanish. And now, I've translated them into English.

Notwithstanding, the careful reader of these stories will gain insight into mythology in general, a look into cultural psychology, linguistics and social anthropology. These stories clearly offer a separation between the study of social anthropology and the study of mythology for the repeated and striking reappearance of motifs that are found worldwide are clearly represented in this collection.

For example, the flood motif, the theft of fire, the moon and his sister, the extraction and playing with eyeballs are all, clearly, not fixed to one culture, so therefore are not the subject of an ethnographic monograph. However, they do give insights into the evolution or development of mythology.

These stories do offer the social anthropologist the opportunity to study the gap between a horticultural society and a modern global super economy. The psychologist could find insights into how culture effects perception and personality. And lastly, the ethnobotanist may see how cultures adapt plants for various uses.

Often in examining the art or literature of a native people. The anthropologist ignores the idea that the expression that he is trying to understand have an aesthetic quality. He sees only as an objective scientist. He does not see the native artisan as would the biographer of Michelangelo. Instead, he sees the native artisan as a person who continues traditional crafts. This view although not necessarily false can be misleading. The Socratic idea that art is what is beautiful and useful, or the ideas of Aquinas that art is what is beautiful because of its divinity, are both still very relevant to native art and literature. In sum, the falsehood that an indigenous community although not in conflict with itself is still in conflict with a large over- arching bureaucratic super economy, and this would produce neurosis or artistic genius ignores the fact that the same environment may produce a widely different experience for the intelligent understanding sensitive individual than for the dullard.

Since the primary author of these stories was Tesere, we can keep Tesere as the focal point for this analysis. The great manifestations of society have in common with works of art that they originate at an unconscious level. They are part of a circular structure of influence between the artist of engineer and the social structures that surround them. They result directly from urgent conditions surrounding the artist. And certainly, Tesere is in a point of great crisis, for the total of his society and culture are about to tragically disappear, and through literature Tesere is preserving his dying culture.

Moreover, the careful reader of these stories will be encompassed by the religious or artistic nature of these stories, for they transcend their story teller and their environment. Taken all together, these stories have a completeness that takes the reader on a journey. These stories are much more than a segment in an ethnographic monograph. They are the essence of a lost culture.

Through the lens of native eyes, we can see ourselves more clearly. And we can look into our world in various ways. We can see these stories as explorations into new frames of mind far out of the normative direction. The stories tell of a people who did not adapt or assimilate but resisted change until the end. Global culture proved unable to control them, and I think that its failure to overwhelm them leaves us with some profound questions about our strength and resilience.

These stories being a kind of ethno-philosophy a philosophy that our philosophy with its great books still can't forbear the loss of the unconscious human connection to the environment. And perhaps this is why western culture has a history of religious intolerance and racism and why such insane savagery continually reappears.

In general, it is important to study the mythology of South America for according to Bierhorst an important authority on mythology. The mythology of South America has been largely ignored, what's been published has not been presented in an appealing readable form. Bierhorst goes on to say that because of the relatively undeveloped interior of South America that South America has conditions for the fresh and vibrant production of mythology. (Bierhorst 2002)

These stories are part of the larger Tupi-Guarani tradition, but they are important differences. Since they were collected by a German anthropologist, they are not included in the literature of American anthropology, and they have been unduly neglected.

The extreme remoteness of the Guarasug'we and the single-minded determination of the Guarasug'we to avoid assimilation helped to develop a unique oral literature. Moreover, the special talents of Tesere gives these stories a special place in the Native literature of the western hemisphere, and it does give us motivation for the study of this literature.

Although the process of cultural assimilation had very much affected the Guarasug'we, and they had abandoned their near nudity and were dressed like mission neophytes or mestizos, the Guarasug'we were proud of their culture and remained defiant until the end.

The Guarasug'we were not insensitive to the customs and morality of their neighbors. Instead, the Guarasug'we were striving to prevent internal moral decay from the neglect of their own principals.

Here I would include this classic Guarasug'we statement collected by Jurgen Riester from an unidentified informant.

We invite you to come into our community to write down our history, before we are all dead. Tell the world that we are not animals. Say to them that we have laws and principals that we live in a community of law and order. We live according to these laws that were given to us by the creator. (Riester 1977)

In summation, these stories are the final lucid expression of a people who no longer exist. Clearly, we must feel the responsibility to treat with care and preserve this last remaining fragment.

Notes on translation

Whenever anyone makes an edition or translation of Native American stories, they are automatically placed within a controversy of whether to present the stories in a prose form or in poetic verse. Very large exhaustive studies have been made and great arguments have been raging between mighty professors. I don't think that I can resolve this controversy, for there are too many unknowns about the speech situation or the stage upon which these stories were performed. Notwithstanding, I will definitely side with those who feel that these stories are, in reality, poetic verse.

Unquestionably, these stories were once poetic verse, for prose is a form of written literary expression that does not exist in cultures that depend upon oral history, and these stories are part of an oral tradition. Since it is now impossible to reconstruct the sage upon which these stories were performed, it only gives truth to the superimposition of a non-intrusive stable poetic form for that would represent what is now lost.

I'm presenting these stories in a free verse form using adverbial and prepositional transitions to mark verse. The verses are long when they seem to be part of a single frame of mind and shortened when they represented sudden shifts of emotion. The sentences or phrases are an imitation of the manner of speaking that Native Americans commonly use.

The translation of these stories presented me with a number of intractable problems. For example, cultures are never static. They are always changing, and the ambiguities expressed in the original text maybe reflect ambiguities of the informant's culture, and the clarification of these ambiguities would distort the informant's expression.

Additionally, religious terms are especially difficult to translate because of their multivariant symbolism. Kinship terms are not universal and vary semantically among cultures. Animal metaphors are often based upon said characteristics of animals that are unrecognized by the general public. The whole concept of culture even at a scientific level is vague and difficult to apply, and grammar doesn't help, for non sensical things can be said with perfect grammar.

Moreover, these stories are translated from a translated text, and the original text has been rewritten and organized. The clarity gained in the text through the editing process may, in fact, contain a severe distortion as it is over simplifying the whole.

Unfortunately, I like so many other experts of Native American literature are only working with existing texts. We excuse this by the fact that broad social and economic change has left little or nothing of many aboriginal cultures, and in the case of the Guarasug'we, the entire culture has disappeared. Yet we assume that aboriginal cultures are unregenerate, and could not exist in a modified contemporary form.

From the moment one defines a culture, it become something else, and any attempt to hold it in place is an attack upon its true life. There is no one true official version of a myth. Mythic time and space are dreamlike an incoherent. Entertainment genres and sacred genres are often interchangeable.

Another set of impossibilities has to do with transformational grammar. There are syntactic units other than words or phrases that are only revealed by intuition. These syntactic units consisting of the interrelationships between words and phrases are often lost in the translation and editing process. Deep and surface structures would have been used differently in the original oral performance than in the written translated form. Certainly, this is a serious loss of meaning.

Lastly, Native American rhetorical devices are not well known or available for use.

In addition to the inadvertent story modifications that are the result of the story passing through the distortions caused by cultural differences, there is the deliberate modifications of the stories. First of all, there are ethical considerations. For example, should the translator translate and include stories that could be used by bigots as a justification for the discrimination against an ethnic group? Moreover, are stories dealing with sexually explicit phrases, stories dealing with torture or cannibalism or other things offensive to the dominant culture fit for inclusion.

Another perplexing problem is the real possibility of plagiarism. Collectors of native oral literature may have taken stories from other native traditions or invented stories and presented them falsely. In this volume, stories such as the ant bear and the jaguar or the moon and his sister are so profoundly similar to stories from cultures as far away as the artic that if these stories were modern fiction, they would be considered plagiarism.

I've written this book not as an attempt to create a work of artistic beauty but rather as an attempt to save the last remnants of a lost culture. However, the attempt to eliminate the subjective may not be in the best interests of the book, for these stories are part of an oral tradition, and the attempt to imitate this might serve the truth. Although care must be taken so that the writer's particular style does not become too apparent. In reality, no matter how objective a writer's style all writing remains essentially subjective, and all writing must be subjective or be nothing.

In general, poetry uses organizing principles to create meaning, and the familiarity with and the use of these principles such as alliteration, repetition, parenthesis, and many more is something to be seriously considered by the objective writer, for the narrative use of language is an as complex of an expression as is the syntax or pronunciation of a language. There are rules for the making of traditional narratives as well as there are grammatical and pronunciation rules for the use of language.

Once when I was talking with a famous paleontologist, we discussed the possibility of dinosaur speech. The paleontologist emphatically stated that dinosaurs could not speak, for they had no vocal cords. Somewhat later, he stated that there were certain dinosaurs who had extensive brain development, and he was unsure of the function of these structures. I suggested that in human evolution the development of larger brains was associated with language development. And it would follow that these dinosaurs may have evolved the larger brain for non-verbal communication.

Such is the complexity of non-verbal communication that so many factors can change meaning. For example, make-up, perfume, textile patterns, colors, time of day, season of the year, weather, sexuality, gestures, tempo of voice, pitch, volume are only a partial list of the almost infinite factors effecting how a message is sent and how it is received. Hopefully, this translation will capture the moment of action the dynamics of the communication.

It must always be remembered that myths are in constant change from speaker to speaker and from situation to situation. The path of meaning is segmented by pauses in speaking and by the alternation of sound and silence. The lines often show an independence of from grammar and even from relevance to the rest of the story. In short, the translator must preserve the mystery or confusion of the situation. Attempts to overly clarify will cause distortion.

The final question for this chapter has to be whether the good translator is objective or subjective. At first, this seems an easy choice, for it is the role of the anthropologist/scientist to describe and present the facts, yet this can cause a terrible distortion, for the anthropologist/translator is not a detached impartial observer, but an influential participant in the story's relationship to the world. Human beings are truly incapable of objectively observing other human beings. And although the anthropologist has the sincere desire, he must be careful not to ignore his own intuition.

Levi-Strauss once wrote that the meaning of a myth comes through in the worst translation. (Levi-Strauss 1967) The worst translations contain the essential meaning, because, in depth, all people have the same psychic structure, and the anthropologist's ego imports a false separation in which his Biblical stories are not as the sacred stories of others of differing religious traditions. And so, makes a false mystification of the sacred oral literature of other cultures and does not write these stories with faith.

The scope of the study

Although my training or education is that of an anthropologist. I'm hesitant to call this study anthropology. The wildly unexpected similarities of mythic themes and motifs among peoples throughout the world makes me think that the study of mythology is more psychological than it is cultural or social.

However, I will proceed with this book as though mythology were largely a cultural entity. I do this more because I feel that this book is urgently needed than because I'm concerned with preserving the bureaucracy of anthropology.

Far from being general, this book is primarily concerned with the translation and preservation of the mythological oral tradition of a very small South American native group. Moreover, the group that to whom these narratives belong no longer exists.

I first came upon these narratives when I was a working in South America as a Peace Corps volunteer. And there, I began to study these myths, for they were entirely written in Spanish, and I was trying to improve my grasp of that language. Surprisingly, I discovered that these myths contained something extraordinary. Although they were, at times, trite and pernicious, taken as a whole they expressed very deep thinking about man and nature.

For the English reader, I believe that there is no other English translation. However, there is a German translation under the title "Die Pauserna-Guarsug'we monographic eienes Tupi-Guarani Volkes Ostboliven" by Jurgen Riester. And there well may be various Spanish versions of these myths, for they are working their way into popular Bolivian culture.

Although there are many impressive studies of myths, there exists no one form of mythic analysis. In this study, I'm not going to analyze myths. Instead, I'm going to let the myths speak for themselves. Clearly, these myths belong to the Tupi-Guarani cultural tradition, for there are motifs and plots that could be found throughout the vast area of the Tupi-Guarani culture area, and I will describe this area shortly.

As for now, I want to emphasize that the culture in the twilight of its existence produced something unique in the world of mythology and leave the mythological overviews to Bierhorst, Levi-Straus, or Joseph Campbell.

The origin and death of the Guarasug'we

The Tupi-Guarani language family is only one 65 language families in South America, but it covers an a very large part of the continent of South America. For example, the continent of South America has three great river systems. Two of these great river valleys were once populated by Tupian peoples. The Tupian peoples who once populated the Amazon from its mouth to the Guapore River have largely been absorbed into mestizo populations.

In contrast, the Tupian peoples who settled the valley of the Rio de la Plata are still there, but they are now called Guarani. The Tupian populations who settled the Atlantic coast are now completely replaced. The area between the Amazon and the Rio de la Plata known as the highlands of Brazil was not part of the Tupian culture area.

The great vastness of Tupian expansion was due to a very functional mode of production. The Tupian mode of production was centered around the cultivation of manioc. However, hunting and, in particular, fishing facilitated a rapid riverine expansion.

The Tupian expansion was often at the expense of many other ethnic groups not only with the conquest of territory but with the cannibalism. Tupian peoples were successful in armed conflicts, but the diverse groups of Tupian peoples never organized into a unilateral militaristic army.

Additionally, Tupian migrations were characterized by a singular concern, or the messianic search for a utopia. The stories presented in this volume are similar to the stories of all Tupi-Guarani peoples. And much has been said of "the search for the land without evil."

The formation of the Guarasug'we

The widely scattered populations of Tupi-Guarani never formed into a state level society, and they fell easily to the Spanish and Portuguese. The Spanish and Portuguese had developed a highly effective organization for the conquest and subsequent enslavement of tribal peoples.

The Spanish were not colonist or pioneers but were conquerors. The first army of army of conquerors to enter the upper tributaries of the Rio de la Plata near present day Paraguay was led by Nuflo de Chavez. This expedition's militaristic conquest was against the Guarani groups who had earlier migrated into the area to raid eastern flanks of the Inca empire.

The Guarani put up fierce resistance to the Spanish, but disease among other factors brought about their defeat and subjugation. (Service 1954)

Afterwards, the Spanish established a Jesuit mission system in the area. This purpose of this system was to transform the warlike Guarani into feudal serfs who would through their agricultural efforts support a Spanish aristocracy.

The Jesuit mission system was highly successful, but the system pursued an independent path, and they came into conflict with the Spanish and Portuguese governments. The conflict developed into war, and as a result the Jesuits were expelled from all of South America. Although the Jesuit missions were immediately turned over to the Franciscan Fathers, the Franciscan mission could never provide the protection of the neophytes that the Jesuits were able to provide from the exploitation by governmental and commercial interests.

The majority of Guarani were incorporated into this mission system, but Guarani groups continued their resistance. In particular, the subject of this study the Guarasug'we remained independent of the mission system by retreating further into wilderness areas.

With the South American independence from Spain and later Portugal, the establishment of the nation of Bolivia, Paraguay, and Brazil separated indigenous peoples behind nationalistic borders. Also, the former powerful mission systems had combined distinct ethnic groups into one complex thus creating new ethnic groups from the mixing of peoples and languages.

With all the moving about and mixing, there came many epidemics and depopulations of indigenous peoples. In this new society, the global influence led to the replacement of traditional ways and beliefs, and the old ways were mostly forgotten, and the new ones not fully accepted and diverse groups of peoples were seeking equilibrium instead of chaos.

Although the progress was slow, the indigenous peoples began to adapt customs that were compatible with the dominant culture. For example, they began to wear clothes that covered the sensitive areas of their bodies.

Notwithstanding that the Jesuits were expelled in 1767, the political power structure that they had built had a revival in Paraguay. And in 1862, this resurgent power again came in conflict with the nations of Brazil and Argentina. This major conflict further separated the Guarani peoples of Paraguay and Bolivia.

The final chapter in the history of the Guarasug'we begins with the Chaco war of 1880. This war erupting from the competition for oil between Shell and Standard oil interest set a pattern of foreign powers being able to exert their business interests unrestrained throughout eastern Bolivia.

Up until this period, the remotest areas of jungle or forest remained in accessible and undesired for development.

Then, the world-wide demand for rubber led the world economy deep into the depths of the tropical forests. This excited search for rubber brought money seekers to the remote area where the Guarasug'we had fled. These profit seekers brought epidemics of influenza and pneumonia that radically reduced the population of Guarasug'we. Also, there was a final unsuccessful attempt to missionize the Guarasug'we

The rubber boom was very intense and it lasted from 1880 to 1945. After 1940, rubber plantations replaced the native trees, and the searching through the forest slowed down. However, in 1945, the price for rubber escalated with World War two and a renewed search for rubber in the wild forests began. The difficulty of penetrating the dense lush forest led to attempts to enslave the Guarasug'we, mostly, by involving them into a cash economy by stimulating their desire for manufactured goods and undermining their independence.

Additionally, there were Guarasug'we who were forcibly enslaved by the rubber seekers. Some Guarasug'we assimilated into Chiquitano populations and a few escaped into the forest. And by this time, the populations of Guarasug'we had dropped below a sustainable level. The institution of slavery continued, and, in 1968, the last band of Guarasug'we separated when their chief was killed by profit seekers.

According to Alfred Metraux, the Pauserna (the term Metraux used for the Guarasug'we) and the Guarayos are the same people. They separated when the Guarayos consented to live on the mission. Metraux believes the Guarayos to have migrated into the area from somewhere in the space now occupied by the present nation of Paraguay. (Metraux 1942)

In contrast, Dr. Riester does not believe that the Guarasug'we and the Guarayos were ever the same people but were always distinct groups. The basis for Dr. Riester's opinion is from glottal chronological evidence. Dr. Riester found that there was more similarity between the Chiriguano (another Guarani group) than between the Guarasug'we and Guarayos. Furthermore, Riester could not find evidence in the oral history of the Guarasug'we of there have been a separation from the Guarayos. (Riester 1977)

The location of the Guarasug'we

To give the reader a precise location of where the Guarasug'we were located is no easy task. First of all, their location was in a remote inaccessible area. Even today, the area is difficult to get to. However, the area is world famous for its natural beauty, and the government of Bolivia has set aside a portion of it as a national park.

Secondly, it is erroneous to pick a point of the globe to show where the Guarasug'we were located, for they were by culture semi-nomadic, and they were by external pressures driven to seek relocation and seclusion.

And finally, the areas that the Guarsug'we occupied are geographically and ecologically diverse. Although I'd never call the Guarasug'we an Amazonian tribe, their final location was on the Guapore River which is an Amazonian tributary. I would not call them Amazonian because they were originally from the area of present-day Paraguay which is drained by the Rio de la Plata.

The final locations of the last two groups of Guarasug'we are along the north eastern border of the present nation of Bolivia. Their location overlaps into Brazil, and it was the Portuguese explorer Gonsalvas da Fonseca who first encountered the Guarasug'we and left written accounts of his discovery. (Steward 1959)

Lastly, the myths draw on a diversity of ecological systems tropical forests, partial forest, swamps, and mostly riparian life zones.

Ecology

To imagine the ecological settings for these stories may be very difficult for those who have never been to South America or even seen tropical scenery. Moreover, it may be difficult to imagine a small isolated area in the middle of the continent.

The location of the Guarasug'we in the middle of the continent creates a location of overlapping ecological zones. Their location is a mosaic structure of forests, swamps, savannas and stone ridges.

The central feature of the Guarasug'we way of interacting with the environment was its use of riparian life zones for hunting, fishing, agriculture, and transportation. An Amazonian like forest extends southward along the river valleys towards the south. This area is intensely dense with vegetation and is impassable except by river travel. The types and kind of plant growth are the most elaborate on the earth.

Further south the river courses come into a semi forested area a mix of broad leaf trees and prairie. Since the entire culture area is south of the equator, it receives a great deal of rain during the rainy season from November to March. The heat and humidity of the rainy season are almost unbearable. However, during the wet season cool winds from Antarctica reflected off the Andes can bring cooler air nearly to the equator.

Towards the end of the rainy season, the rivers become flooded and great swamps appear. In fact, the largest swamp on earth the Pantanal is very near our area of interest.

In contrast, towards the end of the dry season great barren deserts appear. This extreme rotation between the wet and dry seasons makes the area difficult to control and stabilize for agricultural of industrial development, and much of this area is much like it always was.

In the northern most region of the Bolivian state of Santa Cruz near the Brazilian state of Mato Grosso. The government of Bolivia has established the Noel Kempff national park. The Park is situated between the serrania de huanchaca and the Guapore River. (The Guapore River uses the Spanish name Itenez in Bolivia)

Even today the park is remote and difficult to access. And on the parks northern edge was the final location of the Guarasug'we. The Park incorporates the most dynamic tropical scenery. The Park has wild rivers, large waterfalls, meadows, and stone ridges some up to 1500ft tall. The Park has a variety of intact ecosystems, tropical rainforest, tropical dry forest, swampland, and prairies. Plant species number in the thousands, and large charismatic animals such as the red maned wolf, jaguar, greater anteater, pink river dolphins, giant otters, peccaries, tapir, new world monkeys, agouti, deer, poisonous and constricting snakes, caiman, armadillos, giant toads, and a great variety of frogs. Additionally, an infinite variety of birds, insects, and aquatic life inhabit these tropical zones.

The tropics especially the lower elevations were never changed by the last great ice age, and the gradual development of the major South American mountain ranges like the Andes, or the Brazilian highlands did not disrupt evolutionary stability or elaboration. The result is that the tropical rainforest is the most complex of all ecosystems. This makes the presentation of these stories more difficult. For example, these stories in the Spanish do not clearly indicate the species of bird that the story is telling about. The major bird categories could be referred to narrow down the general category of bird, but this is hypothetical work and not scientific.

Human impacts on the ecological life zones of this area were largely European except in the near the area of the Moxos where large hydraulic irrigation system once existed. The first European ecological impacts began faraway on the Atlantic coast, but they quickly spread up the Rio de la Plata with the mission system's agricultural mode of production. The missions were situated near the confluences of rivers where trade could be established with military protection.

Eastern Bolivia and the Brazilian State of Mato Grosso were largely undisturbed until during the rubber exploitation. As world- wide demand for rubber grew, and only old growth forest could supply the demand. This widespread energetic movement left many inroads into the South American tropical forest, and in human terms, many native peoples including the Guarasug'we were enslaved for the production of rubber.

Only recently has the serious deforestation of South America began with major losses to the old growth forest. Wide spread lumbering, mining, and agricultural expansion are the major elements of change.

The Guarasug'we economy

Central to the horticultural economy of the Guarasug'we was the cultivation and processing of bitter manioc. Although this cultigen was Tupian in origin, it is an important cultigen over much of tropical forest areas of South America. The processing of bitter manioc is described the diagram.

Additionally, the cultigens of the Guarasug'we included corn, squash, sweet manioc, peanuts, beans, tobacco, pineapple, cotton, and many more.

The Guarasug'we lived a semi-nomadic way of life. The practiced slash and burn agriculture or migratory agriculture. They would establish new agricultural areas in the forest every two to three years, but these areas circled around a base camp. Older areas ere revisited to harvest perennials like plantains manioc and many more.

Additionally, they gathered wild starches such as arrow root tubers and a vast collection of wild fruits and plants used in their pharmacology. Although the women were usually closer to the gardens, both sexes were involved in hunting and gathering activities.

Although there was some domestication of wild pigs, hunting and fishing were always primary and essential to the economy. Hunting in the tropical forests and prairies requires mobility, for game is sparse and widely scattered. The Guarasug'we would set up hunting camps in order to cover large areas. The women would accompany the men at these temporary camps. There, the women helped in processing meats and transporting supplies in baskets.

The Guarasug'we were skilled hunters, and hunting was considered to be sacred activity. They were keenly aware of the habits of their prey. For example, they hunted tapir during the new moon. They looked for the little Amazonian deer around mango trees, and the agouti near the chonta palm. The Guarasug'we could easily recognize the footprints of any animal in the area.

Equally important their supply of protein was fishing. They used nets, traps, fish hooks, spears, bow and arrow, and poison to catch fish. During the dry season, fish became stranded in pools, and there they were easily caught. Turtles and turtle eggs were gathered on the river banks. And they, also, consumed grubs, insects, and honey.

The practice of cannibalism that was an integral part that was an integral part of Guarani culture at the time of colonization does not seem to have been a practice of the Guarasug'we.

In addition to horticulture, hunting, and fishing. The Guarasug'we gathered wide variety of plant foods that grew with little or no assistance in the areas they frequented. It is especially difficult to verify in translation specific types of plant or animal. Estimates are that the number of different edible fruits they used was around fifty and the number of seeds and tubers innumerable.

The preservation of foods involved drying and storing meat in the rafters of their houses. Manioc was processed into a flour and used while they traveled or hunted.

The Guarasug'we obtained many medicinal plants found in the eco systems that they inhabited. These substances were under the control of a shaman, and he elaborated the use of these substances with rituals and with animal claws, feathers and various others ceremonial objects. An examination of these shamanistic practices is beyond the scope of this book.

Although the Guarani were once a warlike expansionistic power, the large war preparations such as the palisaded villages used by the Guarani were not in use by their offshoots the Guarasug'we. The older complex chiefdoms of the Guarani had disappeared, and their defense against slavers and other enemies was largely a retreat into inaccessible jungle areas.

During the last days of the Guarasug'we their economy was integrated with the economy of the rural mixed- race peoples, and their desire for manufactured goods led them into a life of semi slavery.

Traditionally, the Guarasug'we wore little or no clothing, and they used a wide variety of decorative patterns to beautify their bodies. In particular, they used an orange paint easily obtained from a common bush. During their last days, they dressed similar to the numerous peasants that they were in contact with.

The Guarasug'we family was, also, the basic unit of the Guarasug'we economy. Families usually consisted of one man and one woman living together in a communal house. Some more influential men having several wives. Within these family units they made the tools essential for daily living namely textiles for hammocks and fishing nets. Additionally, they made ceremonial objects and an assortment of musical instruments.

Their material culture included hundreds of small handmade objects, and much larger hunting shacks, family houses, and communal houses. These houses, usually, were made of bamboo poles and palm branches woven together.

Perhaps, the most elaborate and important material procession the Guarasug'we made for themselves was their canoes. These were carefully fashioned from a single tree and through a long intensive labor process, they were brought to perfection. The canoe not only provided access to fishing sites; it was their main vehicle of transportation.

Religion

The principle religious figure of the Guarasug'we is the god Yaneramai. And it is the ultimate goal of each Guarasu to please Yaneramai. Now, Yaneramai is similar to the other principal deities of other Guarani peoples, for he is the master of the land without evil, and he is imagined as a solar spirit and pictured as a benevolent old man or grandfather. He symbolizes the desire to leave this world through natural processes. Reunion with Yaneramai is part of a strong complex of messianic ideas.

Many of the motifs used in the stories in the book are surprisingly universal. For example, the motif of the moon and his sister, and origin of the sun and the moon are very similar to stories told by Thule or Eskimo peoples. And although Yaneramai is credited with causing a flood that covered the earth, stories about great floods that covered the earth can be found in the religious stories of people world-wide. Moreover, stories of twin hero an arch type of two brothers playing a primordial role in the formation of the cosmos is very similar to the Popul Vuh and many other religious stories found world-wide.

The Guarasug'we like smaller organic cultures have an important role for the shaman as a mediator between the spirit world and the tangible world. In Guarasug'we culture the shaman is especially important, for he directs the characteristic migrations in the search for a land without pain and suffering. Moreover, among the Guarasug'we the shaman is a close advisor to the village chief.

In modern society the shaman has largely been replaced by the cleric who is given a strong bureaucratic role very unlike the shaman's charismatic power. In modern society, the shaman is usually characterized as a witch, a paranoid schizophrenic, or a sexual degenerate, for he is not part of the bureaucratic structure and as a free agent is a threat to its existence.

In contrast, the perception of the shaman in smaller organic societies is of a person with special powers. For example, he is generally seen as someone who can speak with the cosmic forces and with Yaneramai. He works as a mediator between the living and the dead. He travels to other worlds in sleep or trance and can catch glimpses into the present, past, and future.

The shaman, also, plays an important role as a healer of sickness. He can see the spirits and material objects that cause disease, and he knows dances, incantations and rituals that can cure sickness. He can, also, suck out diseases. At the time when these stories were being collected, the shaman's power was declining as Christianity took hold.

The spiritual edifice of the Guarasug'we is composed primarily from the subjective meanings that human actors attach to their perceptions and actions within the framework of their minds. In judging the various myths presented in this volume, we need to pay attention to the myths of the greatest psychological assumption, the ideologies, the symbolic images that are accepted by the majority but produced by a minority for either purely selfish reasons or for the functional health of the society or culture. The reader must, also, understand the explorative nature of myth that through myth the human mind can form a structure for the organization of their perceptions of the universal and apply this structure to things yet unseen or felt.

Yet nor every myth serves to reinforce or expand the subjective structure, for contradictory explanations and descriptions are universal to all myths. Even in the symbolic systems of the great religions phrases such as the mystery of the faith are basic to those systems.

It is in the very nature of religion to encompass everyone who reacts to its symbols and to create a solid block with the materials of diverse personalities, and the glue that holds societies together is mythology. Rituals are derived from myth, and myths are ritualistic in themselves, for they are recited in ritualistic patterns. Rituals dissipate the tensions around social transitions, death, marriage, birth, and power transitions. The arts, music, and dancing all serve to elaborate the significance and credibility of a transition.

Sudden transitions such as violent or untimely death happen without rituals to tranquilize the society, and as a result the spirit becomes enraged, and the enraged spirit remains near the sight of the act of violence or sudden accidental death.

The Guarasug'we have a system where by every person has three souls. The profound serata soul, which is always tranquil, and the Yanerataque soul, which is the soul that always seeks revenge for wrongful deaths, and the Muo, who is one's mischievous but good- hearted companion soul.

All of the three souls are mentioned in the stories in this volume, but conspicuously missing are the connections between the stories and the rituals. I suspect that because there were only fifty Guarasug'we in existence at the time these stories were collected that the larger rituals were short of participants for a viable performance and that these stories themselves were the principal rituals of the Guarasug'we in their declining state. (Riester 1977)

The messianic search for a land without suffering is a salient characteristic of all Tupi-Guarani peoples. Its origins predate European contact, and the custom is spread across an immense area of South America. The special mythology that authorizes the messianic migration is incorporated into a wide variety of Tupi-Guarani tribes. An in- depth study of these social movements is beyond the scope of this book, but I'd refer the reader to cantos IA and IB to see how the Guarasug'we were affected by the search for the land without evil.

The modern Guarasug'we version of the search for utopia can easily be divided into three points of view. First, the search as a flight from the encroachment upon native territory from modern development. And this seem very plausible, for their last known location was in an extremely inaccessible area which even today remains remote. Moreover, their isolation would have separated their culture from modern tools, clothing, and Christianity, and this, clearly, would have served to maintain cultural purity or helped to prevent cultural mixing and disintegration from foreign ways of life.

Second, the Guarasug'we migrations could be viewed as a strictly religious practice, for they seemed impelled by some existential need to search for a land that they will never find. The land is no longer a physical place but a place reachable only by death. Their search is prayer, this prayer is an important part of their religion. They search for a land in both real and imagined space that they need to find before the end of the world, so they can be saved. It is a place that only a few can find either in the actual life or in some future life after death.

The third point of view is that the Guarasug'we were in a state of mental confusion. For example, their practice of regular migration was a part of their agricultural methodology. Clearly, migrations have an economic benefit, yet the migrations are, also, a religious practice. The confusion of economic and religious motivations would explain the apparent darkness in which these migrations continued.

Lastly, the direction of the supposed search for the land without evil was towards the west toward the heavily populated coastal areas of South America where it would be highly unlikely that a horticultural society could ever exist.

The Guarasug'we were not fixed into an abstract religious state. They were often inspired by their environment. Yaneramai their principal deity is, clearly, a solar spirit, and the sun is an important focus of their religion. The concept of the moon and the blue jaguar again demonstrates this principal. Myths and rituals dealing with the stars and planets are not so much involved, and this is likely because of the almost constant cloud cover.

The Guarasug'we fear the night and the cool south winds and being alone. They have a female deity an earth mother who gives birth to the animals in clearings in the forest. Certain animals perform supernatural roles such as the red wolf, a large foxlike animal, whose religious role is to transport the dead to the house of the sky. The chuubi bird, likely a harpy eagle, performs a variety of supernatural roles, and the vulture among many other birds play religious roles.

To the Guarasug'we all of the natural ambience that surrounds their horticultural villages is filled with benevolent and malevolent spirits, and these spirits play minor roles in their lives. Their religion is often vague and adaptive with few idols, but with a wide variety of ornaments to attract or repel spirits bird skins, carved fish, claws are just a few examples.

Otherwise, they are fascinated with the spirituality of whirlwinds and river rapids. They make a bright orange mascara from the crushed seeds of a common local bush. And along with eyeliners they paint geometric designs on their faces. They continue these activities regularly.

Finally, something that I personally had a hard time understanding was their concept that the human voice is composed of spittle, and that this spittle can be taken out of the throat and placed outside the human body and then could engage in conversation, yet this concept is not unique to the Guarasug'we, for it exists in Mantaco native literature as well.

A central an important part of the Guarasug'we religion is the practice of hunting and fishing. Although hunting and fishing are more likely to be considered as economic activities, hunting and fishing are part of an intimate relationship between every Guarasu and the cosmos, the environment, the tribe, and the family.

Unlike the large scale Tupian hunts requiring social cooperative organization for war rituals and cannibalism, the Guarasug'we hunts were much smaller with various hunters of a group dividing into solitary hunters and later regrouping.

In viewing the Guarasug'we unconscious assumptions about hunting and fishing a number of important morals appear. First, the hunter must always be careful not to offend the animal's master spirit. These masters of every kind of animal are the protector of that species. These masters of each kind of animal realize that humans need to eat the animals that they protect, but these masters are easily offended if the hunters kill more than they need and do not practice conservation. Moreover, the master expects that after each successful hunt the hunter will perform rites and rituals for preparing and consuming the meat.

Although it is easiest for us to read and evaluate these stories as a member of a bureaucratic super economy, we must try to read these stories in order to see how a Guarasu might see us. We the people of science and the supposed processors of the eternal absolute truth. We are fixed to our cultural points of reference, and we cling to these structures because we fear meaninglessness of powerlessness, yet in our defense of our own culture, we create a destabilizing potential for over-reaction. A wider broader mind is more adaptive to social change. Of particular concern, the environmental crisis that looms over modern civilization has been caused by the attempt to fit the environment into a bureaucratic view of the world.

Overall, it must be remembered that these expressions of Tesere et al that were recorded by Dr. Riester are set in a time of cataclysmic cultural-economic change. We see the dichotomy of the pure group in contrast to the infected group. A true community reduced by disease, nationalism, international religion, and capitalism. The Guarasug'we were surrounded by Catholic missionaries, slavers, rubber tree tappers, Brazilian business men, Chiquitanos, Guarayos, Chiriguano, Siriono, and other native groups, and by large numbers of campesinos.

The ideology of racism, religious chauvinism, and capitalism created the familiar sight found world-wide of a culture of poverty with all its self -loathing and alcoholism, and the creative genius of Tesere is in many ways similar to the creative attempts made through history to heal the deep social wounds.

Social ambiguities

For this final essay, I feel that I must call the reader's attention to aspects of the social situation of the Guarasug'we that may not seem obvious. Despite Dr. Riester's courageous and brilliant attempt to encapsulate the Guarasug'we inside a monographic net, there are important areas where critical information is absent.

For example, Riester's description of the Guarasug'we was done at a time when their numbers were so low that the tribe lacked much of a selection of persons with leadership potential. And a lack of leadership would lead to a disintegration of the culture, for the leader is responsible to preserve and develop rituals and ceremonies and coordinate participation. Moreover, important descriptions of the social processes of the Guarasug'we are absent. For example, he makes no studies of how children were raised or how the aged were treated. There are no studies of athletic competitions or important rites of passage such as marriage, puberty to adult, or baptism. There is no mention made of a calendar.

Otherwise, the literature of the indigenous peoples of south America often includes descriptions of warfare, but little to nothing of that is present in the stories or in Riester's monograph. Additionally, the use of alkaloids, alcohol, and other narcotic substances is never mentioned by Dr. Riester, but Dr. Metraux makes mention of the use of alcohol. (Metraux 1942)

There are few extant photographs of the Guarasug'we, but their being closely related to other Guarani groups one could safely assume that the use of a brilliant orange mascara and feather ornaments common to other Guarani groups were, also, part of the dress commonly worn by the Guarasug'we.

Lastly, Dr. Riester's monograph or the stories of Tesere et al do not give an examination of kinship terms and structure, taboo foods, or the enforcement of behavior mores.

An important and urgent thought when one deals with a particular ethnic group is the problem of group boundaries. Dr. Riester and Dr. Metraux have contradictory views of the boundaries of the Guarasug'we or Pauserna. According to Metraux, (Metraux 1942) the Guarasug'we or Pauserna are not a separate tribe but a sub-culture of the Guarayos. He describes them as simply as Guarayos who would not submit to the mission system and stayed aloof in the forest. The ceremonial traditions that Metraux describes are consistent with the dejection and disillusionment felt by disenfranchised minority groups similar to Oscar Lewis's culture of poverty typology. (Lewis 1963)

Dr. Riester strongly contrasts the Guarasug'we to the Bolivian. However, it seems possible that the Guarasug'we could be just a lot group of people clinging to the illusion that they are not part of a much greater political economic mass of people. The alienation an internal apathy being the impact of the imposition of a powerful social class structure. Maybe, the Guarasug'we were in a transitional stage where their traditional equilibrium had been lost.

Now, other Tupian groups have clearly been successful in becoming separate integrated cultures with a full set of ceremonial activities. For example, According to Reed, (Reed 1995)the Chiripa have developed a successful economy not based upon the enslavement of nature but a cooperative relationship between man and nature.

It could be that the Guarasug'we were never a truly separate culture, and the remaining Guarayos are evidence of the culture's continuance. When one considers the great musical composer Sebastian Bach, we automatically assume that Bach is a voice of all humanity and not just a voice of Germany, yet in the case of anthropological informants, we assume that they are inextricably a part of their ethic group.

For just a moment, let's imagine Tesere et al as a voice for all humanity and not just a native informant from a remote jungle. Now, Tesere like other artists being a marginal individual who by his intimate knowledge of his culture is reflecting upon challenging and criticizing his culture.

The stories that I've translated clearly do not appear to be in broken Spanish or some creole Spanish, but they are in a solid clear Spanish. And so, this leaves me to doubt that a person whose primary language was not Spanish could have written them, so my questions are about the identity of Tesere. Was Tesere truly a Bolivian, or have these stories been radically modified from the originals?

Finally, there are still more inconsistences about these stories, and there is missing information. For example, the collections of oral literature from groups surrounding the Guarasug'we are often presented in a very different manner, for they are lacking much style of symmetry. Moreover, some of these stories seem more like dirty jokes that were never intended to be preserved or taken seriously.

I've tried not to be selective and present all the stories, but I don't understand why some of the stories were ever saved.

Lastly, the dense moist jungles of central South America do not preserve material objects from even relatively recent times, and much less the prehistory. Although this lack of data is not central to this study, it does weaken our availability of information.

Preface

Ideally, it would be better if every anthropologist went out and collected their information from the source, but this has now become impossible as so many of the subjects that anthropologist once studied have been largely absorbed into modern global economies and have simply disappeared. The subject of this study is a sub group of the Guarani Native Americans called Guarasug'we by Dr. Riester and Pauserna by Dr. Metraux. The Guarasug'we no longer exist, for they disappeared in the late 1960s.

Although the Guarasug'we were recognized as a tribe by Fonseca (1880), Nordenskiöld (Reed 1995) (Reed 1995) (1920), and Metraux (1940), Dr. Riester was the only anthropologist to make an exhaustive study of this tribe. Dr. Jurgen Riester earned his PhD from the University of Bonn Germany. In addition to the volume that contained the stories that I've translated and presented in this volume, Dr. Riester's other works include, large works on the anthropology of eastern Bolivia as well as many professional articles.

Dr. Riester completed his doctorial field work in eastern Bolivia, and his sponsoring agency was ACOP, or Aid for the small farmers of Eastern Bolivia. Additionally, he was a professor at the catholic university in Lima Peru.

Dr. Riester's has clearly credited and stated that he is not the author of the stories of which I've translated. He, clearly, names all the actual authors in the footnotes to each story. And I've continued to name the author and the date of the story within this volume.

Dr. Riester published these stories in German, and his German volume was translated into Spanish by an independent translator. And it was from this volume that I translated the stories from Spanish into English. Although these stories have undergone double or triple translation, they are clearly meaningful and authentic in the English volume that I've presented. And I've worked with a great deal of native mythology and discourse. In fact, the subject of my Master's thesis was native discourse. (Nickol 1994)

Although several native story tellers contributed stories for this volume, the bulk of the stories were narrated by a man named Terese. Terese was a middle-aged man with a wife but no children. He lived in a communal house with seven other families. Tesere grew up in a vigorous mestizo culture and could speak Spanish, and he narrated these stories to Dr. Riester in Spanish.

Tesere was uneducated and likely illiterate, but he was keenly aware of social justice. For example, this quote. "We invite you to come into our village to record our stories before we are all dead. Tell the people of the world that we are not animals."

Tesere, Hapik'wa, Jersuu'su et al were well aware that their culture had no future. Formally, there had been many more Guarasug'we, now there were only fifty individuals. This remnant of the culture is so small that it could not be sustainable.

Tesere et al were well aware of the devastating decline of the Guarasug'we, and I think they were interested in the preservation of something of their culture even if only in a literary form. And hopefully my translation and presentation of this extraordinary collection of stories will preserve something of a lost culture. And, perhaps it is important for anthropologists to realize that anthropology is more than history; it is, also, literature.

Cantos in mythic time

Canto I/A

The origin and migration of the Guarasug'we

Tesere and Hapik'wa 12/15/1964

In the beginning, Yaneramai created man from the seed of a puribe. Then, he made the trees, animals, plants, rocks, and water. Then, he taught the Guarasug'we how to cultivate plants and how to use the bow and arrow.

In that time, the Guarasug'we had everything they needed. They processed the eternal light, and there was no evil in the world. Then, Yaneramai went away and left his people to guard the eternal light.

Because of their neglect, the Guarasug'we lost the eternal light. And death and evil came into the world. In time, they lost even the memory of the great father.

Then one day, a great shaman told the people of a land without evil. He told them that he would lead them there. And so, the Guarasug'we followed the shaman to look for the land without evil.

Traveling west, they crossed vast savannahs. They traveled through dense forests and waded through miles of swamps. They crossed many rivers and endured great hardships, but they held fast to their hope of finding the land without evil, for in this land they would find the eternal light, and there would be no more death, injuries, sickness, and the people would have all they needed. In the promised land, there would always be good hunting, honey, and sweet fruits.

After they had traveled a great distance, they grew tired and could no longer travel. And so, they settled down in the land where the Guarasug'we live today. They lost hope of finding the land without evil. This is why we are living in this place. After we die, our souls may be able to arrive at the house of the dead.

Canto 1/b

The migration of the Guarasug'we

Tesere 1/3/1965

In the beginning, Yaneramai lived alone in the darkness. Then he made the earth and balanced it upon two poles. Then, there appeared the great and small worms Maidyeuho and Maiyehim. Now, there were two worms in the darkness with Yaneramai. And from beneath the earth, Yaneramai climbed up a bamboo tree looked about and smiled. And so, Yaneramai came to walk upon the earth in the direction of the rising sun.

In one hand, he carried the seeds of the puribe squash, and within his body he carried the eternal light. He scattered the seeds, and from them came the people. And after the people appeared, Yaneramai created the animals, the plants, the hills, and rivers. Then, he taught the Guarasug'we how to use the bow and arrow to hunt animals.

During the time that our father lived with us, there was no death or evil. The people possessed the eternal light. And our father said to us "guard the eternal light." Then, he traveled west and left us behind.

Afterwards, the people lost the eternal light. And into our perfect world came evil and death. And evil and death are here with us now. And according to our sacred word, Yaneramai destroyed the earth with water from beneath the surface. Only one man and one woman were saved. When the waters retreated, the people returned to the land.

And there arose among them a great prophet, and he told the people "Because you have forgotten Yaneramai, the world was destroyed. If we remain here our souls will be lost, we must go beyond and search."

Under the guidance of the prophet Karaiuhu, the Guarasug'we set out in search of the land without evil. Over vast territories, plains, jungles, and rivers, the Guarasug'we traveled west in search of the land without evil. During their march, they sustained many injuries, but they clung to their hope of finding the promised land.

In time, the Guarasug'we were weakened by hunger, for the lands they passed through were deficient in game, honey, and manioc. In exasperation, the Guarasug'we settled in the land that they are living in at present.

However, the people have never given up the hope of returning to the time when they possessed the eternal light. Now strangers have taken over the land. They have brought us new tools. We have come to depend upon these tools, and now we are lost.

Now, the only way to find he land without evil is to pass through the doorway of the house of the dead.

Canto II

The theft of fire

Tesere 11/5/1964

Long ago in the mythic time our ancestors did not have fire. In that time, they had to eat their meat raw. Sometimes, they dried it in the sun. They had to eat the fruits of the forest in the state that they found them in.

Among the Guarasug'we, there was only one man who knew the secret place of the fire. This man wanted to steal the fire for his people and himself, and this is what he did, and this is the story of how he did it. One day, this man marched into the tall trees, and there he cleared a space. Then, he laid down and pretended to be dead. In time came Uruvusi the white vulture. Uruvusi was the master of the fire. Uruvusi wanted to cook and eat the man, so he gathered up the wood for the fire.

After the white vulture lit the fire, and it was burning. The man jumped up and took a burning ember out of the fire. When Uruvusi saw what the man had done, he called for help from the black vultures "he is stealing the fire! He is stealing the fire!"

Now, the panicked man dropped the ember and ran away. In all the commotion, the vultures did not notice the giant toad hidden in the grass. Carefully, the toad drew near the fire pit and stole three embers. He hid the embers inside his mouth and hopped away.

After a time, the vultures returned to their village. There, they counted all the embers and discovered that there were three embers missing. Then, the white vulture jumped up and quickly returned to the place where the fire pit had been. And there not finding the three embers, he began to search the area.

He saw that the trail of embers led to the village of the Guarasug'we. In pursuit, the white vulture flew up to the giant toad. And he asked the toad "what have you done with my embers? Where did you put them?" And the toad responded "I haven't done anything with your embers. I'm only passing through." And then, the white vulture asked "then why are your footprints so near the fire pit." And the giant toad responded. "I was near the fire pit, and I watched all that was happening, but I did not steal your embers."

And so, the giant toad left with the embers and took them to the village. There, he gave the embers to the people. From that time, the people have treasured fire. They have jealously guarded the fire night and day, and they give thanks to the giant toad.

Although the Guarasug'we have had fire for a long time, sometimes they would lose the fire in their migrations across rivers, forests, and swamps. And when they would lose the fire, they would have to eat their meat raw, or dry it in the sun, and they would be sad.

Then one day, Uruvusi the white vulture came to the people and asked. "Why are you sad?" and the people replied. "We have lost our fire." And Uruvusi replied. "Here I will show you how to make fire. Take a stick and grind the stick into another stick until an ember appears."

And so, the people did this, and from that time they could make their own fire.

Canto III

How thunder and lightning came into the world

Tesere 1/4/1965

In the time before our time, it came to pass that their lived a man and a woman with their three sons. Now one day, this family went into the tall trees to hunt. Since they wanted to hunt for a while, they set up a hunting camp, the woman stayed at the camp, and the man and his three sons went into the tall trees to look for game.

Every night the man would return from the hunt, and he would go and lie down in a small hut with his wife and go to sleep. One night, his wife said to him "come over here and lie down in this pit that I have dug for you." And so, the man went over and lied down in the pit. He didn't think about it, for he didn't suspect anything. And there, he fell asleep.

Then, his wife began to collect the leaves of the pachiula palm, and she made a long basket. And as the man was sleeping, she pushed him into the basket. He did not wake up, for he was sleeping so soundly. Then the woman sealed up the basket with palm leaves, until nobody could tell what was in the basket.

Later, the boys returned from the hunt. They had killed some animals, they divided the meat and gave some of the cuts of meat to their mother, and she put them away. Then, they returned to the hunt, and they killed and butchered many more animals. Then one day, the boys asked "where is our father?" and their mother replied "he was here working on our sleeping hut, but he went back into the tall trees to hunt. I'm sure he will return soon."

And later when the man did not return, the boys asked again. "Where is our father?" and she replied "he is out hunting in the tall trees. I'm sure that he will return tonight or tomorrow." Then, they went to sleep, but in the morning their father had not returned, and they thought "surely he must have returned to the village. We will go back to the village and look for him."

And as the boys were packing for the return to the village, their mother gave them a long basket to carry. The boys were surprised by the weight of the basket, but they said nothing. And when they got back to their village, they looked for their father. Now, the boys were very hungry, and they asked their mother for some food.

And their other went over to the long heavy basket looked at it and said "this meat is not yet ready." And the boys replied "go back and look again." And so, the woman went over to the basket lifted up the palm leaves and went back to the boys and said "the meat is not ready."

Now, the boys did not understand. And so, they went to lie down in their hammocks. They tried to sleep, but they could not, for they were worried about their father. And while they were there resting, they heard a very faint voice, and the voice was coming from the long basket, and they remembered how heavy the basket was, and they thought "our father must be in the basket." Then, they approached the basket.

There, they noticed that there was a small snail shell on the basket. Then, one of the boys put some of his spittle into the snail shell. And the spittle asked "father is you in there?" And a faint voice from inside the shell said "yes I'm in here." And the spittle replied "we are going to get you out."

When they saw their mother coming, one of the boys took out his eye, and put it into the snail shell. Then, the boys ran away. When the evil sorceress arrived, she went over to the basket and said "when are you going to die." And the man replied "I will die soon." And the woman said "hurry up! I'm tired of waiting."

After the woman was gone, the boy returned to the basket. He picked up the snail shell and went into the tall trees. He listened as the spittle told him everything that had happened, and he watched as the eye showed him. And then, the young man took his eye over to the stream to wash it off. Then, he tried to put the eye back in his head but it would not fit.

His brother came along and said "we need to wash the eye again." And while the brothers were washing the eye, a fish jumped out of the water and stole the eye. They tried to catch the fish, but it was too late, so the boy lost his eye.

Then the boy with one eye told his brothers what the spittle had said and of what his eye had showed him. "Our father is locked inside a long basket, and it was our mother who locked him in the basket. We must kill our mother and free our father."

Now the boys prepared to kill their mother. They made a plan to kill her. And when they returned to the village. They gathered up the ashes from the cooking fire and went over to the house where their mother lived. There, they used the ashes to draw four rings around the house of their mother. Then, they hid themselves and waited for their mother to come out of her house.

After a while, the woman came out of the house to fetch some water from the well. When she crossed the first ring of ashes, she fell to the ground and cried "oh why did I fall?" She got up to her feet and walked across the second ring. Then she fell violently to the ground and screamed. She continued on to the third ring. And there, she was thrown to the ground with even greater force. She got up very slowly and crossed the fourth ring. There, she was thrown down with such force that the impact killed her. When the boys were sure that she was dead, they went up to her body and stared a moment. Then they went into their mother's house and pulled the palm leaves off from the top of the basket.

There, they found their father. He was very thin, for he had not eaten since before he was in the basket. As their father climbed out of the basket, he thanked his sons for getting him out, and he said to them "now, we need to get out of this village!" The boys agreed, and the man and his three sons set out with their father. They traveled for many days and nights and across many lands helping many people along the way.

One fine day, they seen a large chonta palm off in the distance. When they got up to it, they saw a carpenter bird sitting on one off the tree's branches sunning itself. One of the boys took out his bow, and he prepared to shoot the bird. When the bird cried "don't shoot me! If you don't shoot me, I will give you something special." The boy put away his bow, and they all watched the carpenter bird.

Then, the boy said to the bird "if your gift is good, we will let you live." Then, the bird jumped from branch to branch until he came near to the fruit of the chonta palm. There he heard the master of the chonta palm cry out "What are you doing there!" and the bird replied "I'm warming myself in the sun." And the master of the chonta palm replied "If you are just out for sun, then what are you doing near my fruit?" and the bird replied "I'm picking off the caterpillars that were eating your fruit."

And the master of the chonta palm replied "all right, but be careful of the fruit." Now, the carpenter bird was ready. He jumped over to the chonta fruit and began eating the caterpillars. Then he put the chonta fruit into his beak, and he flew over to the men and said "here in my beak I have a gift. Give me your arrows." And so, the men gave their arrows to the bird, and the bird pulled them across his beak polishing the arrows with the juice of the chonta fruit.

Now the arrows shone brilliantly in the sun, and they were easy to see when they fell to the ground. And from that time, the Guarasug'we have polished their arrows with chonta fruit juice.

And while they were talking, a toad was watching their every move. And when they were not looking, the toad went over and urinated on the arrows. And where the drops of the toad's urine touched the arrows, it dissolved the chonta fruit juice. Then, the men thanked the carpenter bird and went on their way proudly carrying their beautiful arrows.

They traveled far and wide. After some time, they grew tired and rested on the earth. They wanted to travel to the heavens, so they shot an arrow vertically, and it stuck in the sky. They shot second arrow, and it stuck into the first arrow. Then, they shot a third, fourth, fifth, and many more. And so, there were many arrows hanging in the sky. Then, they climbed up into the sky upon the chain of arrows.

From that time on, they lived in the sky. They became the thunder and lightning. The father of the boys is the thunder, and his sons are the lightning. Up in the heavens, they storm. The father storms about the evil woman, and he commands his sons to shoot their arrows and make lightning.

When the bolts of lightning strike the earth, they shatter into pieces because the toad's urine dissolved the palm oil.

Canto IV

The Origin of the Moon

Tesere 11/3/1964

In the time before our time, there lived a man. Every night he would secretly visit his sister, and have sex with her. His sister did not know who was having sex with her, and she wanted to find out. When she thought of a plan, she carefully set out into the tall trees to find the bi tree. When she found a bi tree, she took some of the black ink and put it into a bowl beside her hammock.

The next night when the man climbed into her hammock for sex, she put her fingers into the black ink of the bi tree, and then she touched his face as he was having sex with her. After the man had left the bed of his sister, he looked into a pool of water and saw that his face was marked.

Now he was very much afraid, and he thought "what if the village finds out that I've been having sex with my sister?" And so, the next day, he climbed to the top of the highest mountain on earth to escape, but he did not feel safe. And the following night, he climbed into the sky and became the moon.

Now the woman continued to look for the man who had been having sex with her, but he could not find a man on earth with black stains on his face.

Then one night when the woman was sitting in front of her shack, she looked up into the sky. Then she saw the ink-stained face of the man who had been having sex with her, and she exclaimed "there! There he is! He is the one who has been having sex with me!" Now the whole village knew the identity of the man, but the man would not return to the earth. He found great advantage in the sky, for he could continue to visit each woman during the full moon.

And from that time, women menstruate after every full moon.

Canto V

The game of the sun and the moon

Hapik'wa 11/3/1964

Now the people do not understand what happens when the sun goes down, and it becomes dark, and they are afraid. The sun disappears from the sky and only the moon is visible, and this happens every day.

Before, the moon would go beneath the earth to play with the sun. They would play for a while. Then, the sun thought that the moon should go to work, and he ordered the moon to leave. The moon was afraid of the sun, for the sun was very powerful. The moon left at once and returned beneath the earth.

And now when the sun sleeps below the earth, the moon shines. And when the moon sleeps below the earth, the sun shines.

At times the sun wants the moon to return, but the moon is gone, and the sun is very sad. Great clouds cover the face of the sun, and you can see the sun's sadness.

At times, the moon comes out to play with the sun but only for a moment.

Then, the moon goes away again.

Canto VI

The Great flood

Tesere 11/3/1964

And it came to pass that there came a man to the villages of the Guarasug'we. He came from the direction of the rising sun. Nobody knew who the man was. Nobody knew that the stranger was Yaneramai. In the villages of the Guarasug'we, Yaneramai fell in love with a beautiful maiden. Although the maiden had no husband, she was not interested in Yaneramai.

There Yaneramai pleaded with the maiden. "I love you please come and be my wife." She responded coldly. "I don't want you, for you are old and ugly." Now the people thought that the maiden had the right to refuse an old man, but Yaneramai became enraged and declared. "I will flood the earth for this insolence, and most of you will die."

Then, Yaneramai took out a stone ax and a club of chonta palm wood, and the people watched in disbelief. And they talked "what does this mean? Why would someone want to destroy the entire earth only because a girl refused him? Can this man do this? Is he as powerful as he thinks he is? We did nothing wrong; we only tried to respect the rights of a girl. If he is really as powerful as he says he is maybe we should grant him his desire?"

And so, they continued to discuss what they should do. And while they were talking, Yaneramai opened great holes in the earth, and water began to gush out of them and flood the earth. Then the mother of the girl who had spurned Yaneramai cried. "The stranger has turned my daughter orange. He is very powerful! I will have him for my son-in-law, so he will not destroy us with water!"

Yaneramai heard what the woman said, and he hesitated for a moment. Then, he spoke in a powerful voice. "Now that I have no need of you! What would you have me do with you?" Then, Yaneramai lifted his arm and the maiden turned into a deer and ran away. Then, Yaneramai called the men together and said to them. "If you want to live, you must come with me to my house, for there is only place you will be able to live."

Very few of the men followed Yaneramai to his house. And when the followers Yaneramai arrived at his house, he ordered them to go up into the rafters and hang up their hammocks and lie in their hammocks and wait.

And when the level of the water rose, those who had followed Yaneramai were saved. Then, Yaneramai closed the doors of his house and climbed to the roof of his house. Again, he commanded the waters to rise still higher.

And so, the waters gushed forth from the holes he had made in the earth. On the second day, the water flowed forth with even greater force, and by the third day the water covered the tallest trees and the highest hills.

Then, Yaneramai took his stone ax and his chonta club and made a hole in the sky. And the waters continued to rise. Those who followed the advice of Yaneramai and had hung their hammocks in the rafters of the great house of Yaneramai stayed above the rising waters. Then Yaneramai called to the birds "fly to my house grab it with your feet lift it up and fly it through the hole in the sky." And so, the birds lifted up his great house and carried it to the hole in the sky.

Then, Yaneramai warned the people. "don't look down upon the depths of the waters, for if you do you will turn into frogs." And those who looked down were turned into frogs. When the birds arrived at the hole in the sky, they could not get the great house of Yaneramai through it.

And so, Yaneramai with great effort enlarged the hole, and the birds carried the house through it. They brought it to rest overlooking the earth from up in the sky.

For a long time, the waters covered the earth. Many weeks passed while the people lived in the house of Yaneramai and ate his food. Always Yaneramai had food, but no one knew where he got it from. Then one day, Yaneramai spoke "let the fruit of the cusi palm fall to earth. Let us go and see if there is still water beneath us." And so, the people gathered up the fruit of the cusi palm and let it fall to earth, but no one heard anything.

Then Yaneramai asked "is there a man who would go down to the earth? And there would he look to see if it is still flooded?" And then a man spoke up. "I will go, and I will look." And Yaneramai warned him. "Go forth down to the earth go and look but don't touch anything, and if you feel hungry don't eat anything, for if you eat or touch anything I will punish you."

And so, the man went down to earth. There he found the earth covered with water and everywhere there were dead animals and no signs of life anywhere. Then, the man became very hungry, and he thought. "I must not eat the dead animals, but if I'm careful no one will know." And so, the man ate the dead animals, but as he was eating, he turned into a vulture. And now, he must eat dead animals forever.

After a few days, Yaneramai asked "is there anyone who would go down to earth to see if it is still flooded." Then, another man spoke up "I'll go there and look." And Yaneramai warned the man "go forth down to the earth, but when you are there, you must not touch anything, and if you become hungry, you must not eat anything, and if you do otherwise, I will punish you."

When the man arrived at the earth, he found that the waters were receding. All the earth was covered in mud, and there were dying fish on the mud, and he could see no living things. And then, he began to walk. After a while, he became hungry, and he ate a little fish. Then, he returned to the great house of Yaneramai. And there, Yaneramai asked him "how are things upon the earth? Is it still covered with water? Did you eat anything when you were down there?"

And the man replied, "the whole of the earth is covered in mud. There are dying fish spread all over it. I swear that I've not eaten anything." And then Yaneramai spoke. "So now the earth is covered in mud. And you have lied to me. You have touched and eaten, so I'm going to change you into a Tuyuyu bird. And forever more, you will eat fish." And so, Yaneramai turned the man into a Tuyuyu bird. Now, he only eats fish.

Then, Yaneramai sent another man down to inspect the earth. He said to the man. "Go down to the earth and look it, but don't touch anything." And so, the man went down to the earth. He found that the earth was almost dry. As he looked around, he saw very little life. And when he became hungry, he ate the fruit of the cusi palm. Then, he returned to the great house of Yaneramai.

There, he told Yaneramai of all that he had seen. Yaneramai asked the man. "Did you eat anything when you were looking around the earth?" And the man replied. "No, I did not touch or eat anything." Then Yaneramai grew angry and yelled "you are trying to deceive me, for I know that you have eaten of the fruit of the cusi palm. From this time on, you will eat the fruit of the cusi palm." Then, Yaneramai turned the man into a spotted jochi. Now, he eats the fruit of the cusi palm.

And Yaneramai sent another man down to inspect the earth. There, when he looked around, he saw more life. He saw forests, prairies, mountains, and rivers. As he walked upon the earth, he became hungry and forgot about Yaneramai's warnings and punishments. And he ate some small rocks and worms. When he returned and told Yaneramai what he had seen he said. "The earth is dry, and there is life everywhere. I've done exactly as you have asked me."

And Yaneramai replied. "You have reported well, but why have you disobeyed my orders? I clearly told you not to touch or eat anything. You will be punished for your lying." Then, Yaneramai turned the man into the carau bird, and now the carau bird eats the shell fish of the river.

"And now in the great house of Yaneramai, there were only two people left. All the other people had been converted into animals. Now, the last two people were a brother and a sister. All of the Guarasug'we are descended from this pair. Yaneramai taught them how to use and make a bow and arrow. Then, Yaneramai went to live in the sky. Yaneramai has forgotten about the people on earth, but we will see him again after we die.

One day, Yaneramai will return to destroy the earth. He will destroy the earth with wind, fire, earth quake, and high water. We must find where Yaneramai is; we must find the land without evil before the earth is destroyed. We must have fear of the destruction of the earth, so we can save our souls from destruction.

Canto VII

The loss of the light

Tesere 12/28/1964

In the time before our time, the Guarasug'we had possession of a powerful light. This light was as strong as a star. Everyone was concerned with the light. Then, Yaneramai gave everyone have a light of their own.

After a short time, the people began to quarrel. "I have the best light." "No! my light is better." "My light is better than either of yours." And so, they quarreled and argued that their own light was best. Then the guardian of the light that was like a star spoke. "Yaneramai has told us not to fight. Everyone has a true light of their own."

Nevertheless, the people continued to quarrel and fight. Then, Yaneramai returned to the earth. Nobody knew who he was, and the people showed no respect for him. And then, the guardian of the light that was like a star spoke to Yaneramai. "Everyone is fighting, but I'm still peaceful." Then Yaneramai announced. "Stop all this fighting!"

But the people paid no attention. And so, Yaneramai took and left with the lights that he had given every person. Only the guardian of the light that was like a star was able to keep the great light, for he recognized and respected Yaneramai. In jealousy, the people expelled the one who possessed the light that was like a star.

He disappeared into the tall trees, and nobody knows where he went. Therefore, we must look for him. And when we have found him, once again we will be contented.

Canto VIII

Darkness covers the earth

Tesere 12/28/1964

Since the Guarasug'we did not respect or listen to Yaneramai, he was filled with rage, and commanded the sun to go under the earth. Only the moon shone in the heavens, and, only, by the by the light of the moon were the people able to see.

Everywhere, there was great confusion. They could not find enough animals to eat. They could not recognize their spouses. They could not plant or tend their gardens, for they could not know the time of the year.

In desperation, the Guarasug'we called out to Yaneramai. "Please return the sun to us. We cannot find animals to hunt or fish to eat. We cannot find our wives, husbands, or children. We cannot plant our gardens or collect fruit from the trees of the forest. Soon, we will die"

Then, Yaneramai took pity on the people. He ordered the moon to go and bring back the sun, so the light and clarity would return to the earth. From that time, the Guarasug'we give thanks each morning to Yaneramai for the gift of the sun.

Yaneramai has given warning and almost destroyed the earth. With the great darkness, he announced the end of the world. Now, we must wait for the next sign.

Canto IX

The Hero Twins

Tesere 2/3/1966

In the time before our time, all the animals were human. And in that time, everyone was alike and everybody spoke the same language.

There, the jaguar men roamed, and the agouti woman stayed at home in the village.

There, the agouti woman cared for the jaguar men. She cooked their meat; she made their hammocks; she made the pottery and took care of the children. The agouti woman was very old and only had two teeth.

At this time, our mother Yanehy was walking upon the earth. In her womb, she carried two boys. While still in the womb, the boys already knew much about the world, and they would direct their mother's paths "you must take this direction. Don't take that direction."

The boys would eat while they were still in the womb, and they wanted flowers. When their mother would feed them flowers through her opening, she would say "here take all of it." One day, the boys demanded a brightly colored flower "we want that flower." And their mother gave the brightly colored flower to them, but they were not satisfied and they demanded "now, give us that flower over there."

The twins would constantly demand things and ask questions. Yanehy would become annoyed with them and scold them through her belly. But the twins persisted, and demanded ever more. They caused their mother to cry out. "Give me some peace and quiet! Your only babies in the womb, and still, you demand everything."

Then Yanehy came to a crossroads. And she asked the boys. "What road should I take? She received no answer, so she asked the boys again. "What road should I take?" Inside her womb, the boys were angry with her for scolding them, and they would not respond.

And so, Yanehy did not learn of the correct path. Her only answer was a vague sullen "over there" from one of the boys, and the other boy said nothing. And so, Yanehy started down the one of the roads, but it was the wrong road.

As a result, Yanehy the mother of the twins came to the house of the jaguar men! Yanehy went into the house. There, the agouti woman exclaimed "why did you come here? If the jaguar men find you here, they will kill you!" and Yanehy replied. "I've taken the wrong road. Could you help me? I have two babies in my belly." And the agouti woman exclaimed "wonderful! I will help you. Right now, you must quickly get out of sight, for the jaguar men are returning. Come climb up into the rafters of this house so that they won't see you."

And so, Yanehy climbed up into the rafters. And the agouti woman said "tomorrow I will return to help you, but for now you must remain quiet." And so Yanehy remained very still and made no sound. When the first of the jaguar men returned from the hunt, he sniffed around and said "I smell meat here. We did not find meat while we were hunting. You must have meat here somewhere."

And the agouti woman replied "no there is no meat here and no smell of meat either." The jaguar man believed her. Then, the second jaguar man arrived. And when the second jaguar man arrived, he sniffed the air and said "there is the smell of meat here. We did not find meat when we were hunting. Do you have meat here?"

Again, she denied it "no there is no smell of meat here." And he believed her. Then, the third jaguar man returned, and he again asked the toothless old woman. "My nose smells meat. Do you have meat here somewhere?" Again, the old woman denied it, and as each jaguar man returned, she old woman convinced him that there was no meat.

At last, the leader of the jaguar men entered the house of the agouti woman and said "there is meat here, for I can smell it." The old woman tried to convince him that there was no meat around. "There is no meat here." He did not believe her, and he began to sniff around. He went from one side of the house to the other.

Then, he sniffed the ladder to the attic. He looked towards the attic and sniffed. Then, he climbed up the ladder and discovered Yanehy. He climbed down the ladder and ordered that Yanehy be brought out to the village plaza. When Yanehy was brought out to the plaza, the leader of the jaguar men commanded "beat her with this club until she is dead." Then, one of the jaguar men took the club and killed her.

Then, they took a knife and Yanerykiy and Yaneryvy appeared. The jaguar men put the twins into a pot and put the pot over a cooking fire. Then, the boys jumped out of the pot and stood on its rim. And so, the jaguar men put them into the pot again, and the boys jumped out and stood on its rim once again. And every time the jaguar men put the boys into the pot, they jumped out again and stood on its edge.

And so, the jaguar men put a lid on the pot to seal the boys inside, but the lid popped off, and again the boys stood on the edge of the pot. Now, the leader of the jaguar men gave the order. "Kill those boys!" Then the agouti woman interjected. "Why not let the boys grow up until they are much more of a meal than they are now? Then, kill them and eat them. Give them to me, and I will fatten them up."

Now, the leader of the jaguar men was pleased by the agouti woman's proposition, and he gave the twin boys to her to raise and fatten.

And then, the jaguar men cut up Yanehy the mother of the twins and divided the meat among them. There, the boys watched as the jaguar men feasted upon their mother and chewed on her bones. Now, the agouti woman was happy, for she had two boys to raise.

Yanerykiy and Yaneryvy grew up quickly. After four days, they could walk about. In a little time, they could shoot a bow and arrow. After six months, they were grown up. The twins were generous, and they brought back much game and shared with the village. The jaguar men no longer wished to kill them, for they were so generous, and the jaguar men no longer needed to do the hard work of hunting for themselves.

Then one day as the twins were hunting in the tall trees, Yanerykiv said. The jaguar people killed our mother; they must be punished. Let's destroy all of them." Yaneryvy was in agreement. Then Yanerykiv made a bridge by laying a tree trunk over a raging river. Then, Yanerykiv said to Yaneryvy. "Go to the village and tell the jaguar people to come and see something special across the river."

Yaneryvy went to the village. There, he said to the jaguar men. "Across the river there is something special." And so, all the jaguar people ran over to the bridge across the river, but one jaguar woman remained behind on the shore. When all the jaguar came to the river they stopped and asked. "Where is this special thing Yaneryvy told us about." And Yanerykiv said to them. "It is on the other side of the raging river. You'll need to use this bridge to get across."

Yanerykiv walked across the bridge, and all the jaguar men followed. When all the jaguar me were up on the bridge, Yanerykiv shook one end of the log, and Yanerykiv shook the other. All the jaguar people fell into the river and drowned. Only the one jaguar woman who remained behind on the shore survived.

In all the kicking and thrashing about that the jaguar people made as struggled for their lives, they splashed mud all over the jaguar woman who was standing on the shore. This one pregnant jaguar woman is from where all the jaguars that are living today have descended, and all those spots of mud that were splashed upon her became the spots that jaguars now have on the coats.

Then, the twins returned to the village. There, they found the agouti woman. Yanerykiv and Yaneryvy did not hate this old woman, for she had saved their lives. The boys began to play with the old woman. They took places and began to toss her back and forth between them. After a while, the old woman had enough of this and started to run away.

In that moment, Yanerykiv and Yaneryvy changed the old woman into a spotted agouti, and to this day the spotted agouti still has the spots of the jaguar. And because the jochi woman had been so old, the spotted agouti only has two front teeth like an old woman.

Now, Yanerykiv and Yaneryvy were all alone in the village of the jaguar men. Here, they looked for something to do. They felt free to wander into the tall trees. There they found where the jaguar men had tossed the bones of their mother. And Yanerykiv started to cry. Yaneryvy asked him "why are you crying? What is it that makes you so sad?" and Yanerykiv replied. "I'm thinking about our mother. Here, they tossed her bones. We are nothing without her. No man is complete who does not have a mother. Let us collect her bones."

Then, the boys put all the bones of their mother into a pile. Next, the boys called out to the pile of bones. "Bring our mother back to life." Then, the bones began to gather together and form into the shape of their mother. And then, their mother came back to life. Yanerykiv and Yaneryvy ran over to their mother and cried out. "Mother your alive! Mother!"

Then, their mother fell to pieces, and a voice cried out. "You must wait." Once again, the boys called out to the bones of their mother, and the bones swirled around in a circle, and Yaneryvy ran toward them crying. "Mother! Mother!" Once again, a voice called out. "You must wait." Once again the bones began to fly around in a circle. And this time, Yaneryvy, the elder brother, held his younger brother back.

Then, the bones Yanehy gathered together, and her visage appeared. The impetuous Yaneryvy jumped up, and she disappeared. And a voice spoke out. "Now, you will never see your mother again, for she is gone forever. We gave you three chances, but you were too impatient."

And so, the boys walked sadly away, and for a long time they wandered over the earth. The foolish Yaneryvy made many mistakes, and Yanerykiv corrected them. They were good to all people. They made many things. They made the plants, trees, water, and mud. They gave us the bow and arrow, or that is what my father told me, but other Guarasug'we have a different story.

After they had finished making many wonderful things, they disappeared into the west and towards the sky. There, they joined Yaneramai. Then, they became stars.

Canto X

How tobacco came into the world

Tesere 12/29/1964

Long ago in a time before our time, lived a man and a woman. They were not happy together, and the man wanted to kill the woman.

After thinking about it for a long time, the man thought of a plan for how to kill her.

And so, one day, he said to the woman. "Come let us go into the tall trees. And there, I will hunt, and you can collect firewood."

And so, they went out into the tall trees.

And when they had come to a certain place the man said. "Here we will get started, go and collect the firewood, and I will look for game, and after I return, we will roast the meat, so you need to make a grill and put the firewood under it."

Then, the man prepared his bow and arrows and went into the tall trees, and the woman collected firewood and prepared the grill.

After a long time, the man returned. He had killed a wild pig and had cut the meat into four parts.

Then, he lit the fire, and from a short distance away, his wife watched him.

Suddenly, the man grabbed his woman and tied her feet together with the fiber twine of the peki plant.

Next, he threw her on the grill.

In a short time, the woman was dead.

Here, he let her body burn on the grill till it was nothing but ashes. And when the fire burned out, he returned back to the village.

There, his mother-in-law asked him. "Where is my daughter?" and the man replied. "She went into the tall trees to gather firewood and did not return. I did not see where she went, for I was out hunting. I thought that she was only delayed and that she would return shortly with firewood."

For two days, the old woman waited.

Then, she asked her son-in-law. "Where is my daughter." And he replied. "I have already told you that she went to gather firewood while I went hunting. Maybe, something has happened to her."

And so, the old woman waited another night.

Then, she went into the tall trees to look for her daughter. For three long days, she looked for her daughter and found nothing.

And in time, she came to the place where the fire pit had been. And she sat down to think; she felt that she would never see her daughter again, and she started to cry.

Then, she heard a voice say. "Mama why do you cry? And the old woman replied. "Where are you, my daughter?" And the voice said. "Here I am, in the ashes of the fire. My husband murdered me, and I want my revenge. Will you help me?" And the old woman replied. "Yes, I'll help you.

Then, the old woman began to weep still more.

After a while, she collected herself, and she asked. "What do you want me to do?" And the soul of her daughter said. "Return to the village, and tell no one that I'm dead, and do not grieve, for I'm still here. After the first rain, come back to this place and gather the plant that is growing out of my ashes. Then, take the leaves back to your home and dry them over the fire or just let them dry out in the fresh air. Next, roll the of the plant together, and then lite the end of the rolled leaves with fire, and give it to your son-in-law. Make sure that he put the tube of rolled leaves between his lips and sucks in the smoke. This will be my revenge, for within the tobacco plant there is a power that will enslave all men, and all men will feel my death."

Then, the voice stopped. And the old woman swore "I will do as my murdered daughter has asked." She returned to the village. There her son-in-law asked "Did you find her?" and the old woman sobbed. "No. I could not find her. I'm sure that by now she is dead."

After the first rain, the old woman went out into the tall trees.

There, she collected the leaves of the plant that grew in the ashes of her daughter, and she brought them back to her house.

There, she dried the leaves of the plant, and she rolled them into tubes and gave them to her son-in-law to smoke.

And her son-law- law smoked all them, he felt a deathly sickness, and he tried to stop smoking them, but he could not.

Then, he made rolls of the leaves, gave them to his friends, they smoked them and could not quit, and they gave rolls to all their friends. Soon, the tobacco plant was everywhere.

Now, the murdered woman has her revenge.

Canto XI

The north wind

Tesere 1/15/1965

The north wind is a very powerful giant. He is much more powerful than us.

In the time that existed before our time.

In the time when Yaneramai walked among us, the north wind was much more powerful than it is today.

When the north wind went out to hunt, he would kill many men and animals, he would blow down tall trees and destroy the houses of our villages.

And so, the men of our villages became very angry, and they demanded. "Let's kill the north wind, for he is destroying everything."

And so, the men went out to kill the north wind.

There, out in the tall trees they waited for the north wind to appear.

After a time, they could hear him coming, and they hid in the under bush and waited for him to appear.

When the north wind appeared, they could see that he was an enormous man with a large tree trunk in his hands, and he was using the tree trunk to knock over the trees.

Then, the hunters came out of hiding, and they attacked the north wind man. They took the tree trunk away from him and used it to beat him into the ground.

And so, the hunters believed that they had killed the north wind. They took the tree trunk he used back with them and kept it.

Now that the north wind was dead, they rested in peace.

In time, the north wind slowly rose back out of the ground and blows again.

Now, the north wind is not as powerful as he once was.

Occasionally, the north wind will blow strong again, but this only lasts for two to four days.

The surazo wind

During the hot summer a cool southerly wind blows up the spine of the Andes mountains it goes almost up to the equator. This strange cool wind called the "surazo" can quickly lower temperatures from a very muggy 95 degrees Fahrenheit to a cool 40 degrees Fahrenheit. This strange wind is the subject of the legend of the south wind.

Canto XII

The legend of the south wind

Tesere 1/19/1965

Once upon a time, the cool summer wind began to blow, and two strange men came up to a woman as she was working in the manioc field, and they said to her. "We have come to invite you to go fishing with us, for we think that this is a good time." And she responded. "Where did you come from? What are you doing here?" And the men lifted up their arms and pointed towards the south.

Then, they asked her again. "Would you like to go fishing with us?" And she responded. "No. I have no desire to go fishing, but my husband would like to go. I will go and tell him."

Then, the woman turned to leave, but she turned back to the men and asked. "Is it possible to go fishing when the south wind is blowing? Is it not a foolish endeavor to fish during the time of the south wind?" And the men replied. "We have already thought about that, and it's nothing to be concerned about. Go and tell your husband to come over here."

And so, the woman said no more and returned to her village.

There, her husband was out in front of their house making a bow and arrow. And she went up to him and spoke. "Out there in the manioc field there are two strangers. They wanted me to go fishing with them, but I have no desire to go. You go and fish with them." And her husband responded. "What! Fishing at this time! Can't you see that the south wind is blowing?" and she answered. "I told them that but they insisted that it was a good time to fish, and to ask you to come along. Maybe you will be lucky, if you go fishing with them."

And so, the man and the woman went out to the manioc field to talk to the two men, but the men were no longer out there.

And so, the man and the woman returned home.

There, the woman said to the man. "I'm sure that those men are already at the fishing pond. Now, go after them and bring me back enough fish for supper."

Slowly the man went over to the pond, for he had no desire to go fishing.

Moreover, he thought it was very strange to be fishing during the south wind.

He went out toward the fishing pond, but he sat down by a tree trunk and tried to pass the time.

Then, he was pulled towards the fishing pond by some irresistible force that he could not escape. He tried desperately to hold on to whatever he could, but the force drawing him towards the pond was far too great, and he was filled with terror.

When he came to the pond, both the strangers were waiting for him.

There, they told him. "We have waited long enough. Now, we fish. Sit down right there next to the water and fish." And the man replied. "Why fish at this time? It is not right to fish during the south wind. Only a fool would fish, at this time." And the strangers replied. "Just sit down and watch us."

Then, they dove into the pond and disappeared beneath the waves.

Once again, the man tried to get away, but he was unable to leave, for he was held in place by something strong.

There, he remained seated watching the waving water and wondering where the strangers had gone.

Then, the man saw something black in the water.

Next, the blackness spread out over the water like the whole muddy bottom of the pond had risen to the surface.

Then, the strangers appeared with their arms full of fish. They placed the fish up on the shore and dove again and again into the black muddy water. Each time they reappeared with armloads of fish and placed them on the shore.

Now, the man had never seen so many fish before. And then the strangers said to him. "You see how we fish. Let's prepare a feast. Set up your grill and start the fire. Come join us in a feast." And the man replied. "No! Not right now! I'm not hungry." But this was not true, for the man was hungry but he was afraid to eat the fish of the two strangers.

Then, the strangers insisted that the man eat with them, and the man's hunger overpowered his will to resist.

And so, he put a piece of the cooked fish into his mouth, and at the moment it touched his teeth it turned into a piece of charcoal. He said nothing and continued to eat.

Now! He was lost, for he had eaten the food of the two strange men, and he could never be the same again or ever return home.

Then, the strangers said to him. "Come with us to the south." And the man replied. "I have a wife and children here, and I don't want to leave them. What would I do farther south?" And they told him. "You have eaten our food, and now you belong to us. You must come with us to a new land. There, you will find many women. Here, your woman will find another man. Your children are grown and don't need you."

Now, the man felt changed. He no longer felt human. And he said to the strangers. "I would like to go and say good-by to my woman." And the strangers replied. "Yes. We will take you to her." And so, they lifted the man into the air and brought him before his woman.

There, the man said to her. "I'm going south forever. You made me go fishing during the south wind, and now I'm lost forever! Look at what you've done!"

Then, the woman started to cry. She begged for her husband, but it was too late. And the strangers took him into the south wind.

Since that time, the strangers have returned every year, for they are the cool surazo wind.

Sometimes they are here for only a day. And if there are three strangers, they stay for three days.

Sometimes, one of the strangers will stay a while longer, but they never stay more than four days.

Let us all take warning. During the days of the south wind, no one must walk outside. No one must fish in the ponds or rivers or hunt in the tall trees, for the strange spirits of the south wind will carry them away. Everyone should stay in their house.

And there, do what work they can.

Canto XIII

The origin of the genital organs

Tesere 1/4/1965

In the time before our time, the people had no genital organs. And they thought nothing of it until one day when they watched a macaw copulating with his female.

Then, the people were sad, for they wanted to create progeny.

When our grandfather Yaneramai came to visit them, they said to him. "We want to make children. Help us to make children." And Yaneramai thought. "They need to have genital organs."

Then, Yaneramai went away and after much time, he brought to them the genital organs of the male and female.

At the time Yaneramai returned with the genital organs, the people were having a celebration, and they were not interested in the genital organs, for they understood nothing of their use.

And so, Yaneramai had to wait for the festival to end.

When the festival was over, Yaneramai carefully placed the genital organs in their proper place.

But by then, the organs had started to decompose, and that is why they stink.

Canto XIV

The origin of war

Hapik'wa 12/1/1964

A small toucan was flying over the tall trees, and it was a beautiful sight.

Now, the great master of toucans Sakuahuda was admiring the sight, and he exclaimed. "How beautiful my little bird looks as he flies towards the sun! How delicate and precious he is." And the toucan responded. "Jai! Jui! Jai!"

Further away, some men were watching and taunting the toucan. "Why do you come here just to scream? Why do you come here when your master is over there?"

Then, the took out their bows and arrows and killed the little toucan.

Now, Sakuahuda was enraged by this cruel killing of his little toucan, and he took out his bow and arrows and killed the men.

Next, the families of the slain men attacked Sakuahuda.

Then, the family of Sakuahuda came to his defense.

Now, there was war. The cycle of attack and revenge had no end, and it continued to grow as each side attempted to do greater harm to the other.

Then one day, a wounded man was lying in agony. He had been left to die, as his enemies went to pursue others.

As he lay dying, a group of children came upon the man.

There, the children said. "Let us kill this man, for he is not of our kin-ship." They took out their arrows and prepared to shoot. The dying man called out. "Don't shoot! If you let me live, I will help your group."

Now, the children had no leader, and they were considering the man's offer. And while they were discussing what they should do, a scarlet and blue macaw flew over them, and the boys took out their bows and arrows and shot down the macaw.

Then, they burned the macaw feathers and from the ashes they made a poultice and put it on the man's wounds.

Then, they carried him over to a clearing in the tall trees and placed him where the wind would blow over him.

And so, the wind healed the man's wounds, and when he was fully re-covered the man became the advisor to the group of boys.

Then, the man and the boys avenged those who had killed his kin. He was a good fighter, and the boys learned a great deal from him, and like a true leader he was constantly vigilant and always prepared.

And so, war came into the world. All because of the killing of a small toucan. War is now a part of our world, and no one can escape from it.

Canto XV

The fight against the monsters

Tesere 12/1/1964

And so, it came to pass that the hunters were going into the tall trees never to return. All the hunters were petrified with fear. The terror of the unknown kept the hunters out of the tall trees.

Then one day, a hunter declared. "I must go out to hunt, for we have need of meat."

And so, the hunter went into the tall trees.

Now, in the tall trees were two black jaguars. They would attack and throw the hunters to the ground and drag the injured bodies to their lair.

When the black jaguars saw the man, they captured him and brought him back to their lair and gave him to their cubs to play with.

There, in the lair of the jaguars, the hunter waited for a chance to escape. After the two black jaguars went out to hunt, the hunter got up looked about.

There, he saw a tiny jaguar cub so small that its eyes were unopened. He looked towards the back of the lair.

There, he saw the bones and left-over parts of the hunters that the jaguars had tossed aside.

Then, the hunter ran away from the lair of the jaguars and returned to the village.

There, he told the villagers what he had seen. "There are two black jaguars, who having been killing our hunters, and they have a lair, in the tall trees, full of the bones and parts of the people they have killed."

And so, the hunters decided to kill the black jaguars. They prepared their bows, arrows, and spears. They erected a scaffold to defend themselves, and they went forth to the lair of the black jaguars.

When they arrived, the man with the loudest voice called out to the jaguars. "Here I am come and eat me." A black jaguar jumped out the cave came after the man, but the man was very fast and ran behind the barrier.

There, the hunters killed the black jaguar.

Next, the man went over to the jaguar's lair again and yelled. "Now, you can eat me. If you can catch me." Then, the second jaguar came out of the lair at great speed, but the man escaped behind the barrier.

There, the hunters killed the second jaguar.

And so, the people were free of the menace of the black jaguars, but they forgot about the tiny jaguar cub, and from this cub all the jaguars of today are descended.

Although jaguars still exist today, the hunters have no fear of them, for the jaguars of today understand arrows and spears.

Canto XVb

The fight against the destroyer of gardens

Tesere 12/1/1964

Once there was a wild beast who lived in a hole in a tree. The beast would always destroy the gardens of the Guarasug'we.

And so, the hunters decided to kill the beast. They went out into the garden, and they hid in the banana trees and waited for the beast to appear.

And in time, the monster dropped from out of the tree and went to eat in the garden as it had been doing.

And when the beast started to leave the garden, the hunters killed it with their arrows.

Now, the hunters were content, for they had killed the beast, but they forgot about the little beast that was still hiding in the tree.

Until this day, the beast lives in holes in the trees.

Now, only rarely do they destroy gardens because they remember the bows and arrows of the hunters.

Canto XVI

The conquest of the great chuubi bird

Tesere 12/1/1964

Once upon a time, a great chuubi bird lived alone above the tall trees. He often perched upon the tallest tree. Every time a hunter drew near the tree, the great chuubi bird would circle over him.

Then it would swoop down and grab the hunter in its claws and carry him off to its nest.

There, it would kill the hunter and then devour him.

Now, all the hunters were afraid of the great chuubi, and they were afraid to go into the tall trees to hunt for meat.

Then one day, a brave hunter spoke up. "I will go and kill the chuubi bird."

And so, he went into the tall trees.

There, he laid down at the base of the great tree of the chuubi and pretended to be dead.

When the great chuubi bird saw the man lying there, he flew down and grabbed the man in his claws and carried him up to his nest at the top of the great tree.

And when the chuubi bird was looking away, the man jumped up and killed the great bird.

Then, he made a rope and descended down from the top of the tree.

When he returned to the village, he announced. "I've killed the great chuubi bird. Now, it is safe for the hunters to return to the tall trees."

And in gratitude to the hunter for their freedom from the chuubi bird, the people appointed the hunter to be their first chief, for he was the bravest of them all.

And from that time, every chief is appointed in respect to their meritorious deeds.

And so, it is the way of the chief that he is the strongest, the most knowledgeable, and a fearless protector of the people. He is one who sleeps little but thinks a great deal.

Canto XVII

The man and the vampire bat

Tariku 12/11/1964

Once upon a time, there lived a man who never stopped hunting and working in the tall trees.

When the man was not at home, another man was with his woman. This went on for a long time.

Although the man knew that his wife did not love him, he did not know that she had a lover. He was very sad, for he wanted her to love him.

Then one day, he was hunting in the tall trees, and he met Mopy the king of the vampire bats. And Mopy asked him. "Why are you so sad? It pains me to see your sorrow." To this the man replied. "My woman does not love me. Maybe, she has a lover, and I love her." And Mopy answered him. "Your woman does have a lover, and whenever you go hunting, she is with him."

Then, the man screamed. "How can I have my revenge?"

And so Mopy explained. "Take a fresh sliver of bamboo sharpen it, and hide it under your coat. Go and hide near your house. When, your woman's lover appears, stab him in the penis."

And so, the man followed Mopy's instructions. He made a sharp sliver of bamboo, and he waited to ambush his woman's lover.

And when that man appeared, he stabbed the man in his penis, and the man bled to death.

And after that, the man wanted nothing to do with his wife. He left her and went to live with the vampire bats.

Now, all men must be careful and cover their penises when they sleep, for a vampire bats are waiting to stab their penises and drink their blood.

Canto XVIII

The Pikui bird's tricks

Tesere 12/19 and 20/1964

In the time before our time, all the animals were human, and everyone spoke the same language.

In that time, the trickster Pikui changed himself into a bird, he was a mischievous man with both good and bad intentions.

At times, the rascal would dance in front of a person with something he had borrowed, and then he would run away with it.

Often, he was a thief.

However, he did many good things. He often brought food to the people. If a hunter was injured, Pikui would carry him back to his village.

Now, it is the time to tell of the tricks that Pikui played. How he bamboozled the master of swine, the great bird Mutun, the jaguars, the armadillo tatu, and the master of fire.

One fine day, Pikui went to the home of Tadahuda the master of swine. Pikui found the home deep in the tall trees.

There, he walked right inside and spoke. "Good day Tadahuda" and Tadahuda responded. "Good day Pikui. Would you like something to eat? I have some pork. I'm sure that you must be very hungry." Pikui refused the food and replied. "Thanks for your offer, but I prefer to eat the meat that I've hunted for myself." But Tadahuda insisted. "Be reasonable this is the best meat. Now, come and eat this fine pork with me."

Again, Pikui refused. "No. I prefer to eat the meat that I have hunted." Again, Tadahuda insisted. "You are not going to eat the finest meat! It is far better than any other meat. Now, come and eat this fine pork with me." But Pikui was adamant. "No. I prefer to go and hunt for myself. Give me your weapon, and tell me how you call to the wild pigs."

Then, the master of pigs relented, and gave way to Pikui's request and spoke. "I'd be happy to give you, my weapons. They are a bow and arrows, and I call to my pigs by saying come to your master."

Then, he called to the pigs, and they appeared. And Pikui exclaimed. "Now show me how to shoot the arrow!" And the master of Pigs demonstrated the technique.

Then, Pikui said to the master of pigs. "I can shoot the arrow with the bow, but I don't think that I can call to the pigs so that they will come to me. Let me take your little boy with me so that he can call and make the pigs appear."

And so, Pikui and the master of pigs sat down to talk it over. Pikui pleaded. "I will take good care of your son, and he will call the pigs for me. He knows how to do it, and I will be there to protect him. Please, lend me your son." Tadahuda responded. "He is very small and can barely walk." Pikui assured Tadahuda. "I will carry him, and I will help him each time."

And so, Tadahuda the master of pigs let Pikui take his baby boy.

Then, Pikui and the baby vanished into the tall trees.

At first, Pikui carried the boy upon his shoulders, but when he became tried, he put the baby on the ground and said to him. "Walk by yourself! Why do you think you have feet?" And the baby replied. "I'm still a baby, and I'm not ready to walk." Pikui scolded him. "You are ready right now."

Then, the baby stood up. When the baby did not move, Pikui pushed him, and the baby fell down. The baby raised himself up again, and Pikui pushed him towards the tall trees.

After they had traveled a little way, Pikui said to the baby boy. "We will stay here and call to the animals."

Then, Pikui build a platform up in a tall tree and climbed into it, and Tadahuda little boy called out. "Lift me up on to the platform." And

Pikui responded. "No. You stay below and call to the pigs." And the baby cried. "They will eat me! Please! Lift me up on to the platform." And Pikui replied. "Shut up." Now call to the three jaguars." The boy did not call.

Then, Pikui turned his bow towards the boy and spoke. "If you do not call to the three jaguars, I'm going to shoot you."

Then, the boy called. "Come here your master calls you. The master of pigs is calling you. Come here. Calling all jaguars."

Then, all the jaguars appeared, but none of them harmed the boy.

Then, Pikui told the boy. "Call to all tapirs."

And so, the boy put a hollow stick to his mouth and called. "Come here the son of Tadahuda calls you." And soon all the tapirs came, but none of them harmed the son of Tadahuda.

Then, Pikui commanded. "Now call out to the coatis, agoutis, red wolves, water pigs, porky pines, Brazil cats, deer, monkeys, caimans, black jaguars, and all the birds. Call to everything in the tall trees."

One by one, all the animals appeared and gathered together under the tree, but none of them harmed the son of Tadahuda, nor would any of the animals threaten him.

Pikui thought for a moment. He commanded the boy. "Call to the wild pigs!" And when the wild pigs appeared, they tore the boy apart and ate him.

Then, Pikui went on his way, and when he met up with Tadahuda, he said. "Your son and I were up in a tree, but when he called so many pigs came that I was overwhelmed, and I could not protect him. I'm very sorry."

And so, Pikui went on his way looking sad, but when he got a short distance away, he shouted at Tadahuda. "Now, your son is dead. You are a stupid fool. I wanted him dead."

Then, Tadahuda went after Pikui, but Pikui was too fast. No one can run as fast as Pikui, and soon Tadahuda gave up and went home.

Then, Tadahuda told all the animal people how Pikui had tricked him and caused the death of his baby.

Here, Tadahuda said to the wild pigs. "Vomit up all the pieces of my son, all the bones, all the meat, all the blood."

And so, the wild pigs vomited up all the parts of the son of Tadahuda.

Then, Tadahuda commanded the parts and pieces of his son to come together, and all the bones, flesh, and drops of blood rose up into a gory whirlwind.

Here, Tadahuda commanded. "Spirit of life return to my son." And all the pieces of bone, drops of blood, began to make a roar, and all the animals ran away. The great roar continued until the last piece of the son of Tadahuda flew into place.

And so, the son of the master of pigs returned to life, and he ran over to his father and cried. "Pikui murdered me!" And Tadahuda replied. "Don't worry any more my son, for all your parts have returned, and if I ever see Pikui again, I will kill him."

Now, Pikui had many other adventures, and we will learn of the adventure of Pikui with the master of birds Mituda.

And so, one day as Pikui was flying through the tall trees, he saw Mituda, the master of birds, busily drying some meat. Mituda had shot many birds, and he was cutting them up and drying some of the parts in the sun on a grill.

Pikui looked at Mituda and asked. "Since you have a lot of meat already, would you lend me your bow and arrows so that I might get some meat?" And Mituda responded. "Why would you want to go hunting, for I have plenty of meat already cut up and cooked to share with you?" And Pikui replied. "I want to get my own meat. I don't want to eat the meat that you have prepared. Will you lend me your bow and arrows?" And Mituda said. "Okay, take my bow and arrows."

Then, Mituda, the master of birds, gave Pikui his bow and arrows, but Mituda knew of Pikui's treachery, and he had an idea of how to destroy him.

Now, Pikui was very happy, for he had tricked Mituda out of his bow and arrows.

Then, Pikui said to Mituda. "Tell me where all your birds are so that I will be able to find them."

Then, Mituda responded. "Follow the trail directly in front of you. And when you come to the place where to where two trails intersect take the trail that arches across. This is the trail of the master of birds."

In truth, the trail that Mituda directed Pikui to follow was the trail of the jaguars.

And so, Pikui went down the trail thinking to himself. "Mituda is such a fool. Now, I have his bow and arrows, and I'm going to kill all the birds. Mituda will be master of nothing."

Next, Pikui came to the intersection of the trails, and he took the jaguar trail.

Soon, a jaguar spotted him.

Now, Pikui could not see the jaguar, for he was hidden in the bushes. The jaguar could see that Pikui carried the bow and arrows of Mituda. And the great cat crouched down low so that he would not be seen.

And so, Pikui traveled on unconcerned.

Then! The jaguar leaped upon Pikui and pulled him to the ground.

Then, the jaguar roared. "What luck! He walks right into our village! We finally have him! Now, we will put an end to his mischief."

Then, the jaguars came out of there village. They bound Pikui's hands and feet. And for all his wit and guile Pikui could not untie the bonds.

Then, the chief of the jaguars announced. "Tomorrow we will kill and eat him." Pikui thought and thought about how to escape, but he could not think of something.

Then he heard the jaguars talking. "We must kill him with a club."

And so, the jaguars came and carried Pikui to the center of the village.

And still, Pikui could not think of a plan of escape. The leader of the jaguars said. "Go and get the club and kill him."

And so, a jaguar went and got a club and brought it back.

Then, Pikui cried. "Wait! I want to say something. I want to be killed by an unsuccessful hunter so that he can say that he has, also, made a successful kill." The leader of the jaguars agreed and spoke. "Yes, this would be a good thing." And so, the most foolish warrior came forward. Now, Pikui thought. "How can I make my escape from these bonds?"

Then, the leader of the jaguars spoke. "Give the club to the foolish jaguar man so that he can kill Pikui."

And so, the club was handed to the foolish warrior. The foolish jaguar prepared to give Pikui the death blow, Pikui spoke. "If he were to kill me before he had loosened and adjusted my bindings, it would be difficult to untie me after I'm dead."

Then, the leader of the jaguar men spoke. "Yes, it would be a smart thing to loosen his bindings before he is killed."

And so, the foolish jaguar man went up to Pikui and loosened his bindings.

Then, Pikui jumped up and ran away. All the jaguars pursued him, but Pikui is the fastest runner, and the jaguars could not catch him.

There, Pikui made fools of the jaguars. Jaguars are a stupid animal.

And as Pikui was traveling through the tall trees, he did many kind things. He stopped and helped a poor tried old woman carry her basket. He saved a baby from taking a nasty fall. He cured a sick animal.

Then one day, he came to a place where a large tree was growing. All around the large tree an armadillo had built scaffolds up to where there was a large honeycomb.

Then, Pikui drew near the scaffold and asked the armadillo. "Can I climb up your scaffolds?" And the armadillo replied. "No, I'd prefer that you didn't."

And so, Pikui watched as the armadillo continued to go about his business.

After a while, Pikui said. "Come give me your ax, and I will help you work on your scaffold, for you look very tired."

Now, the armadillo thought a moment and replied. "Okay, you can use my stone ax, for I'm very tired, and I need the help."

Then, Pikui took the heavy ax and hit the tree.

Then, thousands of angry bees flew out of a hole in the tree.

Then, Pikui cried out. "Look out they are coming right towards you."

When the armadillo jumped out of the way, he tipped the scaffolds over.

There, Pikui thought it all very entertaining. And he thought to himself. "Now that the armadillo is dead, I can have all the honey for myself." But the armadillo was not dead, and he had crawled away into a hole.

After satisfying himself with honey, Pikui went to sleep. When he awoke, he thought about the armadillo's woman. He went out to look for her, and when he found her, he told her. "I'm afraid that your husband is dead, but don't be sad, for I'm a man, and you can sleep with me."

Then, the armadillo appeared holding a club, and he tried to kill Pikui, but Pikui jumped out of the way.

Then, Pikui ran into the tall trees. The armadillo chased him, but Pikui is the fastest runner.

In his rage, the armadillo swore. "I will kill him! I will have my revenge."

After many moons had passed, Pikui returned to the house of the armadillo.

And there, he found the armadillo sleeping.

Now, Pikui thought. "This would be a good time to kill him but that would not be as good of a thing as if I were to kill his woman that would serve him right."

Then, Pikui went to find the armadillo's woman.

After looking for her a long time, he found her up on the tree scaffold collecting honey.

Then, Pikui said to her. "This scaffold is poorly made. Would you like me to steady it for you? Look here, the support rope is broken." Now, the woman was delighted to have Pikui help her, and after Pikui had fixed the rope, he asked. "Would you like more help?" And she replied. "Yes, I very much would."

And so, Pikui climbed up the scaffold and said to the woman. "Give me your stone ax. I'm sure that with this ax I could make an improvement."

And so, the woman handed the stone ax to Pikui.

Then, Pikui took the stone ax and struck the tree.

Then, thousands of angry bees flew out of the tree. And Pikui cried out. "Look out they're coming right towards you!"

Then, Pikui pushed her off the scaffold.

And as she was falling to the ground, Pikui felt sorry for her and covered her with a shell to protect her, and when she hit the ground, she was not killed, but she became an armadillo like the armadillos that we know today.

Here, she fell near a hole in the ground, and she crawled into the hole.

From that time on, the armadillos have lived in holes in the ground. The armadillo is a stupid animal, and even women can hunt them. They are so stupid that the armadillo's female did not suspect Pikui when he climbed up the scaffold. She was so stupid that she trusted Pikui even after she had watched him almost kill her mate.

Now, we will hear of Pikui's next adventure with Tatdada the master of fire.

One fine day, Pikui saw the master of fire.

There, the master of fire was knitting a cap out of flames of fire. And Pikui went over to him and asked. "What is it that you're doing?" And the master of fire replied. "I'm knitting a cap out of fire?" And Pikui asked. "Can I help you?" And the master of fire replied. "Yes. You can help me. Would you like to wear this cap of fire?" And Pikui exclaimed. "Yes, I certainly would."

Then, Tatdada gave the cap to Pikui.

When Pikui took the cap from Tatdada, he put the cap on his head, and he began to dance.

Then, he danced in circles around the master of fire.

And as soon as he completed one circle, he would begin a larger one. The spiral continued to grow.

Then, Pikui cried out. "The cap is burning my head!" But the master of fire only laughed.

Now, Pikui was desperate, he tried to remove the cap, but the cap grew tighter and tighter. The cap was burning up all his head. Pikui rolled upon the ground and jumped into the water, but the fire could not be put out.

Then, the body of Pikui began to burn. And all the animals came to watch as his body turned to ashes.

Then, the animals gathered the ashes together and tossed them into the river, and as soon as the ashes touched the water, they changed into Pikui birds.

And from that time, the Pikui bird lives near the water. He is always around lakes, rivers, and streams, and he only eats fish.

And there, you can still hear the sound of Pikui's laughter.

Although Pikui was consumed by fire, he lives on as fire, for sometimes fire is our friend and sometimes our destruction.

Sometimes it burns the tall trees during the dry season, and other times it burns the grass of the plains.

Canto XIX

The story of the baskets

Tesere 1/28/1965

Long ago, there were baskets that would carry themselves. These baskets had legs of their own. These baskets were very helpful, and they made life easier for everyone.

At times, the baskets needed help, for they were not always able to get around obstacles in their path. If they came to a tree in their path, they would wait for assistance.

One day when the baskets were full, and they were trying to go forward. They came to tree trunk, and there they waited for assistance.

There, from down in the under-brush a small taracore bird began to taunt them. "Why are you stupid baskets helping the people? Don't help them. Make them carry their own baskets." And the baskets replied. "No, we like helping the people and carrying their baskets for them."

Then, the taracore bird took a stick and broke all their legs.

And so, the baskets could longer rise up and carry their cargo."

Now, the people heard the baskets cry out, and they came to help them, but it was too late.

Then, from out of the tall trees the taracore bird taunted. "From now on you will have to carry your own baskets."

Then, the taracore bird flew deep into the tall trees all the way singing and dancing. The men pursued him, but he was too fast.

Then, the women spotted a peroto tree, and they took the fibers from beneath the bark and wove them into a belt with a buckle in front, so they could carry the baskets. We men are fortunate that we did not find a peroto tree, for if we had, we would have to carry the baskets.

Canto XX

The birth of the Jaguars

Tarekuve 10/3/1964

Once there lived a woman who had no husband. She had to care for herself and help her brother. Every day she went into the tall trees to look for fruit, and, afterwards, she would go and work in the fields.

Then one day as she was looking for fruit, she met a jaguar man. And the jaguar said to her. "You have no husband, and I have no woman. Would you like to be my woman?"

Then, they joined together, and they became a couple.

In a short while, she was with child.

Then, there came the pain, and she cried out for help from the midwife. "Please! Help me I'm having a baby."

And so, the woman and the midwife went into the tall trees and prepared for the birth in the ancient way.

When, the baby was born, the midwife cried out! "It is a jaguar!" And she ran away and left the woman alone in the tall trees. The midwife returned to the village.

There, she told everyone what had happened.

Now, the woman was left alone in the tall trees to raise the baby boy jaguar.

There, she died, and the jaguar man and the baby boy jaguar were very sad. The little jaguar grew into manhood and took a mate, and they had many children, and from those children come all the jaguars that live in the tall trees today.

Now, jaguars are the enemies of people, because people rejected their mother. The people should have treated their mother better.

Canto XXI

The Origen of the Pink River Dolphin

Hapik'wa 28/11/1964

Once upon a time, there was a brother and a sister living together. They lived among us, there, in the same house. Neither the brother or sister were married. The brother, only, worked to help his sister, and she, only, worked to help him.

Then one day, when the brother was out working in the tall trees, his sister brought him his lunch, as she did every day. This time when she brought him his lunch, he complained. "Why have you brought me so little?" And she replied. "We don't have any more." To this he responded. "I brought you plenty meat yesterday!"

And so, the brother continued to complain about the amount of food his sister was bringing to him.

Then one day, he thought. "Something must be going on. I'm going to spy on my sister and find out what's happening."

And so, he began to watch her.

Then, he saw that his sister was taking food to a tree trunk.

There, she would strike the tree trunk, and, in a little while, a tapir man would appear, and she would give him food.

Then, they would lie down together.

Now, the brother knew what was happening, and the reason why his sister was bringing him so little food.

And so, he went home, but he said nothing to his sister, but the next day, he went to the place where his sister was meeting the tapir man.

There, he struck the tree trunk, and the tapir man appeared.

Then, he killed the tapir man and cut off the tapir man's testicles and hung them in a tree.

Next, he dug a hole and put the tapir man's body into the hole and covered it up.

When the sister returned to give the tapir man food and have sex with him, she struck the tree, but the tapir man did not appear.

There, she stuck the tree again and again.

Then, she looked upward, and, there, she saw the testicles of the tapir man hanging in the tree.

Now, she knew what had happened, and she ran away broken spirited.

In time, she gave birth to the child of the tapir man. She took the child to the river, and jumped into water.

There, they turned into pink river dolphins, and, to this day, the river dolphins enjoy the company of men and always try to play with them.

Canto XXII

How the little deer got its horns

Tesere 1/24/1963

Once there was a man who hated his son.

Often, he thought. "How can I kill my son?"

Then one day, he came up with a plan.

And so, he said to his son. "Come let us go into the tall trees, and, there, we can hunt."

And so, the man and his son went into the tall trees.

After traveling for some time, they came upon a takuapari tree. And although it was getting late in the day, the father ordered his son. "Climb up that tree and bring down its fruit for your mother." And the boy replied. "But father, I'm too small." And the father replied. "I'll give you some help. I'll climb up the tree, and carry you with me."

And then, the father picked up his son and climbed up the tree.

There, they loosened the fruit and let it fall to the ground.

When they were done, the father climbed down the tree and left his son alone sitting in the tree.

And so, the man left his son stranded up in the tree. And he thought. "The boy will not be able to get down from the tree, and there he will die."

Now back at the tree, the boy began to cry. "Father, you are not helping me."

For a long time, the boy cried out, but he received no answer, and his father just returned to the village.

There, he told his wife. "Our son is dead. He was suddenly attacked by a jaguar. I could do nothing to stop the attack."

Then, the man looked very sad, and he started to cry.

And soon, his wife started to cry.

There up in the tree, the little boy sat all alone thinking. "What will I do? If I stay up in this tree, I am going to die."

Then, a small deer came passing by the tree, and the little boy called out. "Oh, little deer, if ever you were human listen to me, and help me."

Then, the urina said. "It is certain that now I'm not human, but I do speak and understand your language." And the little boy exclaimed. "Would you please help me?" And the little deer replied. "What is troubling you?" And the boy replied. "It is my father, for he has left and abandoned me up in this tree. He told me that he needed me up in this tree to help gather fruit, he carried me up here, but, then, he abandoned me, and I'm too small to get down from this tree on my own."

Then the little deer spoke. "Surely, what has happened to you is wrong, and I'm going to help you. I'll come up the tree and sit beside you, and you can climb upon my back, and I'll carry you down to the ground."

And so, the little deer went up the tree and sat beside the boy, and the boy climbed upon the back of the urina, and it brought him down to the ground.

There upon solid ground, the boy asked the urina. "Will you help me find justice?" And the little deer replied. "I will help you, but I need to have horns." And the little boy replied, I'll help you to find horns."

And so, the little boy killed a variety of small animals and left their bodies to rot in the sun.

And so, the boy killed some small animals and left their bodies to rot in the sun.

Then, the smell attracted a flock of vultures. And the vultures cried out. "Give us some meat." And the boy replied. "You can have this meat, but first help my friend and give him some sturdy horns." And the vultures replied. "We can do this easily."

And so, they flew away and returned with horns made of chonta wood, but these horns broke to pieces as soon as they landed. And the boy called out. "These horns are too weak."

And so, the vultures flew away again. They returned with horns made of tajibo wood. When the boy struck the tajibo wood horns against a tree, they broke. And the boy said. "These horns are not strong enough."

And so, the vultures flew away once more in search of a stronger material.

When they returned, they returned with horns made of cuchi wood.

And when the boy struck the chuchi wood horns against a tree, they did not break or even crack. And the boy exclaimed. "These horns are very good. Take all of the meat you want."

And so, the vultures ate all wanted, and the boy fixed the horns upon the little deer.

Now, they began the long journey back to the village.

There, they found the boy's mother weeping.

When she saw her son, she said in surprise. "I thought that you had been killed by a jaguar, yet you are alive. How can you still be alive?" And he replied. "I did not die because this little deer helped me. Father wanted to kill me, so he abandoned me up in a takuapari fruit tree. Now, I've returned to take my revenge against father. Will you help me?" And his mother replied. "I'll help you. What would you have me do?" And the boy replied. "Go and tell father that there is a small deer out in the trees."

And so, his mother went and found her husband and spoke. "There is an urina nearby out in the tall trees."

And so, the man prepared his bow and arrows and went out to hunt the urina.

Out there in the tall trees, he looked all around.

And when he turned towards the little deer, the urina charged him and drove his horns of chuchi wood into the man.

Now, the boy had his just revenge, and the boy and the little deer gave the man's dead body to the vultures.

And from that time, our people do not hunt the little deer, for he is our friend.

Canto XXIII

Why we have mosquitos

Tesere 1/3/1965

In the time before our time, an old woman and her grandson lived alone out in the tall trees. They had no place to stay in the village and never left the tall trees.

Whenever a hunter came by the old woman's house, she would say. "Come into my house and rest."

Then, she would offer the hunter something to drink and eat and invite him to rest in her hammock, and her grandson would talk softly to them.

After they had fallen asleep, she would ask them. "Are you sleeping?"

And when they did not answer she would club them until they were dead.

Then, the old woman and her grandson would cut up their bodies and put some of the meat outside to dry in the sun, and some out it they would eat for supper. Whatever meat was left over they would store the up in the rafters.

Now, the people of the village were getting alarmed by how many hunters were disappearing. They thought a monster lived in the tall trees, and the hunters were afraid to go hunting.

Then one day, a hunter came to the house of the old woman, and like before she invited him into her house or something to eat and drink, and like before she invited him to rest in her hammock and talk to her grandson while she prepared honey corn drink and manioc cake.

And like the other hunters before him, he accepted her invitation, for he was very tried.

After he had eaten, he laid down in her hammock.

Then, he noticed that grease was dripping from the rafters, and when he looked up, he saw meat up in the attic.

And so, he asked the boy. "What kind out meat do you have up in your attic?" And the boy replied. "We have human meat up there." And the hunter exclaimed. "Where did you get this meat?" And so, the boy explained. "When a hunter comes by grandma invites him in for sweetened corn drink and manioc cake, and, then, she invites him to lie down, and after he falls asleep, she clubs him to death, and, then, we cut him up dry the meat in the sun, cook some of it for supper, and store some of it in the rafters."

Now, the man knew why the hunters were disappearing. He wanted to run, but he could see the old woman returning with the honey drink and manioc cake. She offered the refreshments to him, and he took them, but, only, pretended to drink.

Then, he lied down in the hammock, and he pretended to sleep.

And, when, the old woman was out of sight, he got up and put sticks in the hammock and covered them with blankets.

Then, he ran away.

When, the old woman leaned over the hammock and asked. "Are you asleep?" She received no answer, so she went to get her club to kill the hunter. But to her surprise, he was not there only sticks of wood.

When the hunter returned to the village, he said to the people. "Out there, in the tall trees, there is an old woman and her grandson. They invite hunters into their home and give them refreshments and invite them to lie down and rest. After they fall asleep, the old woman clubs them to death. Then, they cut up their bodies dry the meat in the sun and store it in the rafters. They are eating our people! They must be killed!"

And so, the men of the village went out to the house of the old woman and her grandson.

And as the hunters closed in on them, the old woman and her grandson ran into their house.

Then the men of the village set fire to the house, and it burned while the old woman and her grandson screamed.

Afterwards, the men returned to clean up the ashes.

Then, they threw the ashes into the river.

When the ashes fell on the water, they turned into mosquitos!

And from that time, there have been mosquitos in the world, they steal the blood of human beings.

They are like the old woman and her grandson.

Canto XXIV

The son of the Jucumari (a benevolent spirit of the tall trees)

Hapik'wa 1/1/1965

One bright day, a hunter came to a place where there were great hills of solid rock.

Now, the hunter was very curious about this odd place, and he started to investigate.

Then, underneath a large rock the hunter saw something interesting, and he moved in to take a closer look.

Then, a great snake sprang out from beneath the rock and grabbed the hunter and pulled him under.

There, under the rock the snake had a large den.

In the den of the snake, there were many fine things. There were brightly colored feathers, bows, baskets, pottery, and many more wonderful curious things.

Then, the snake said. "I will not kill you, if you do as I say." And the hunter replied. "What would you have me do?" And the snake hissed. "Nothing! You will be my love."

Then, the man turned into a snake and became the lover of the snake Jucumari.

Under the rocks they lived together.

After a time, the snake Jucumari gave birth to a small snake.

Now, this snake grew very rapidly, and it loved its father very much, but the man was not happy, but he could not escape, for every time that Jucumari would go out to hunt, she would place a great stone in front of the door to her den to prevent the man from escaping.

When she returned, she would bring him meat.

Many times, he tried to move the stone, but it was far too heavy.

There under the stone, the three of them lived for many moons.

Every day Jucumari would go out to hunt, and she would return with meat.

Now, the little snake grew bigger and stronger every day.

Then one day, the man said to his son. "Help me push aside this stone that blocks our doorway."

And so, the man and his son pushed aside he great stone.

Then, the man and his snake son fled into the tall trees.

When Jucumari returned, she saw that the great stone had been moved, and she knew that the man and her son had escaped.

And so, she set after them.

Now, the man and his snake son found a cave within the hills of stone. And the man said. "Here we can make our new home"

And as they were clearing the cave of rocks and debris, the powerful son lifted up a great stone and flung it from the cave. The stone fell upon Jucumari and crushed the life from her.

And so, the man and his son went back to the village of men.

There, the people recognized the man and his son as kinfolk and accepted them into the village. They told the people all that had happened to them.

And so, the son of Jucumari the snake woman and his father built a hut and lived in the village.

Now the people of the village loved the son of the snake woman, but the son of Jucumari left the village, and this is the story of why he left and where he went.

Although the son of the snake woman loved the people and wanted to help them, his great strength would bring trouble. He would demonstrate how to use a club, but his great strength would kill some-one. And when he went to gather fire wood, he would pull an entire tree out of the ground and cause the death of someone nearby. And if someone asked for water, he would go and get so much water that it would drown someone.

Now, every time the son of Jucumari accidentally killed someone, he would feel great sadness and remorse and cry intensely.

Then one day, with a look of resolution the son of snake woman said. "I can no longer live here, for I make everything bad here. I'm too strong to live among the people of my father. I'm going out into the tall trees to live, for that is what I must do."

And so, he left the village of his father's people and went into the tall trees.

From that time, he lives out there.

Whenever people are lost or need direction, he, always, helps them. Never does he demonstrate his great strength to those who have never seen his power.

Now whenever the earth shakes, the people wonder if it is the son of Jucumari.

Whenever, they find the strength to uproot a tree, they wonder if it was the son the snake woman who gave them the strength.

Cantos of spirits and souls in the present time

Canto XXV

How the Guarasug'we came to the gully of the dead

Tesere 11/28/1964

In the time before our time there lived in a village of our people a brother and his sister. The brother had a very large penis much larger than other men. And his sister had a very large vagina so large that no penis could fill its enclosure.

And it came to pass one day that the village chief wanted all the single people to choose a spouse.

And so, he announced. "Will all the single people please come into the village so that each one can be matched with someone."

Then, all the people came into the center of the village. All the single men chose a spouse, and the brother with the very large penis chose his mate, and the sister with the large vagina was chosen by a young man.

Afterwards, when the brother with the large penis put it into his chosen mate, he killed her. And the young man who had chosen the sister with the large vagina could not ejaculate inside her vastness.

The following day, the village chief took the brother and sister into consul. "Young man you have killed a woman with your large penis. Young woman you cannot satisfy a man. Therefore, it is my decision that the two of you cannot live amongst our people. Hereby, you are banished from our village."

And so, they left the village and traveled towards the west, and when they came to the place where the dead pass through the hole in the sky.

Here, they sat down by the shore of the river of the dead.

Here, they are still waiting for the people to arrive.

Whenever, a male soul comes by, he will have sex with the sister, and whenever a female soul comes along, she will have sex with the brother.

For after dying, the dead have changed, and they can find great pleasure in the enormous gentiles.

Canto XXVI

The power of the shaman

Tesere 11/28/1964

Among us, the shaman has the power to cure sickness. The shaman consults with the dead and with the masters of animals.

Out in the wilderness, he will wait for the spirits of the earth, land, and sky to draw near.

Then, he speaks to them, for only a shaman knows how to communicate with the spirits.

And so, it came to pass that a man and a shaman went into the tall trees.

After, they had traveled a distance the man began to complain of hunger. "Let's go back, for I'm hungry." And the shaman replied. "I will go and get you food, but you must wait here until I return."

Now, the man knew that he must never watch a shaman when he goes into the wilderness, so the man did not watch the shaman but waited patiently.

There out in the tall trees, the shaman went up to a tree and spoke. "Oh! master of trees, will you help me, for my friend is very hungry?"

Then, the tree opened up its bark and carefully took out some plantains and handed them to the shaman.

Then, the tree closed up its bark.

And so, the shaman brought the man the plantains. The man quickly consumed the plantains, and he spoke. "I'm still very hungry, and I need more." And the shaman replied. "I will go and get you more to eat, but you must wait here."

And so, the shaman went into the tall trees.

There, he called to a fire fly. "Show me where there is a termite mound." The fire fly flew over to a termite mound.

Then, the shaman spoke to the master of termites. "Excuse me your leadership, but my companion is very hungry." The termite mound opened up, and the shaman went inside, and from inside the termite mound he brought out manioc and sweet potato.

Now, you know that the shaman can speak with the masters of all there Is in the tall trees, the prairies, the swamps, and mountains. The shaman can find food everywhere. The shaman is always good to us.

Canto XXVII

Yanerataque Returns

Tesere 12/15/1964

Once upon a time, there was a man who processed two women. The two women hated each other.

Then one day, the younger woman secretly put a lethal poison in the food of the of the older woman, and the older woman died.

Now, the man did not realize that the older woman had been murdered.

After the funeral, the man and the younger wife returned to their home.

There, she cheerfully began working. He thought. "She shows no signs of grief. Could she have murdered my older wife?" The man was very concerned.

Then, he went out into the tall trees.

There, he began to plead with Yanerataque the avenger. "Oh! Please don't return avenger. Spare my household!"

And while the man pleaded with the avenger, the younger wife was in the family house.

There, she was making manioc flour. Yanerataque appeared grabbed the young woman and threw her into the fire.

As the man was returning home, he heard the most terrible voice of Yanerataque the avenger.

Then, he knew what was happening. He ran to find help, and a group from the village came back with him, but they found nothing but the ashes of the young woman.

Now, the soul of the young woman was with Yanerataque, and he carried her spirit up to the house of the dead.

There, both women are together.

Canto XXVIII

The man who met the shadow spirit Yaneague

Tesere 12/15/1964

And so, it came to pass that a party of hunters set forth into the tall trees for their need to supply meat for the village.

But there was one hunter who did not wish to be part of the hunting party. And this hunter said to the others. "I'd prefer not to join this hunting party, for I wish to work, here, in my garden. And the party of hunters replied. "It's better that you join our hunting party, for no one can accomplish anything alone." Yet the man insisted. "I'm sure of what I want to do. Now, go and leave me.

And so, the hunting party left, and the man went into his garden to work.

And there while he was working, he saw Yaneague the shadow. Yaneague was coming towards him screaming with his arms raised. The man ran into the tall trees, and the shadow ran after him grabbing at him, and, almost, touching him.

There, Yaneague was screaming. "I'm going to kill you. Once, I catch you. I will kill you. I will catch very soon."

Then, man found a hole in a tree.

There, he stayed keeping very still.

When Yaneague caught up, he could not find the man.

There in the hole in the tree, the man held very still.

When Yaneague caught up, he could not find the man, and the man remained very still. Yaneague called. "Where have you hidden yourself? You were here a moment ago."

There, Yaneague snooped around the tree, and the man remained very still even though he was covered from head to toe by fierce stinging red ants.

Then, Yaneague quit looking and went away. The man climbed slowly out of the hole in the tree and went back home.

When he returned to his village, he said to the people. "Yaneague tried to kill me. I ran for my life and hid in a tree full of fierce red ants who stung me many times." And the people replied. "You should have gone out with the hunting party. Working alone is never the right thing to do."

Canto XXIX

Yaneratague returns again

Tesere 12/15/1964

A long time ago, our people not only ate the flesh of animals, we, also, ate human flesh, for it was mild and flavorful.

Now, we are civilized and do not practice pagan customs.

One fine day, a man went into the tall trees. He carried with him his bow and arrows.

After traveling a while, he came to a small pond.

As he sat down by the pond to rest, a group of strange men appeared. He took out his bow and prepared to shoot, but before he could the men shot him.

Then, they finished him off and prepared his flesh and ate it.

Now, Yanerataque went into the man's village.

There, he found the man's wife and children, and he told them what had happened and that the man no longer lived.

Then, the avenger of the unquiet dead became pale and started speaking in tongues. The woman became frightened, and she grabbed the children and ran out and hid in her neighbor's house. All of the village could hear the terrible sounds of Yaneratague, and everyone thought that he would destroy the village.

Then, the people of the village watched as the murdered man's spirit left the house. His head was drooping, and in his hands, he carried a trumpet, and he played the trumpet as he walked away along a trail that led towards the setting sun and the house of the dead.

Now when the woman returned to her house, she found that nothing had changed.

From that time, the people have known the ways of Yaneratague, and the people leave the area when the shadow spirit Yaneratague comes, for this is better.

Sometimes when death comes, the dead don't want to leave the earth because they don't want to abandon their families, so they return in an altered form, and return to their houses. They are sad to leave their homes, as they start their journey to the house of the dead.

After they pass through the hole in the sky, they find the river of the dead, and they follow the river until they come to the house of the dead.

There, they seek Yaneramai.

Canto XXX

The death of the Muo

Tesere 12/16/1964

Once there was a man who was always being visited by the Muo. And during their many visits, they would sit and drink and then go hunting.

Then one day, the Muo came complaining of a stomach ache. "There are sounds in my stomach that I can't understand." And so, the man put his ear over the stomach and listened and spoke. "There are foods in your stomach that are not digesting. Do you want me to help you?" And the Muo replied. "Yes, help me. I'll come back tomorrow."

Now, the man was very tired of the Muo, and he wanted to kill it, so when the Muo returned the next day, the man said. "I will look for the enec snake. The snake will eat the rotten food in your stomach."

After the man found an enec snake, he put it up into the Muo's anus.

Then, the Muo gave a cry of pain, and, later, the Muo died from the damage that the enec snake did to his intestines.

And so, one of the Muos who inhabit the earth passed away. All the Muos only live for a time upon the earth.

There, they take the form of an animal at night, and they take the form of a human in the daytime.

Afterwards, they die.

Canto XXXI

A visit to the house of the dead

Tesere 11/19/1964

Here, in a village of our people, there lived a man and a woman.

After a time, the man became very sick and soon died, and the woman was very sad. She continued to cry, and her crying never let up.

Then one day, the woman went out to work in her garden.

There she began to cry.

From his perch atop the tall trees, the chuubi bird could see her crying, and he asked. "Why do you cry? I can see your sadness. Is there anything that I can do?" And she replied. "My dear husband is dead, and I'm filled with grief." And the chuubi replied. "I can help you. Would you want to go to the place where your husband has gone?" And she replied. "Yes, that's what I want, and I want this more than anything.

And so, the chuubi bird told her. "Wait here. I will go and return with my son-in-law; he can carry you to the place where your husband is." The great chuubi bird was silent for a moment.

Then, he said. "It is a dangerous place that place where your husband has gone. They do not welcome the living. Those who live there have everything they want, and they are protected by Yanerataque. And she replied, I have no fear of Yanerataque the spirit of the shadows. Please, bring your son-in-law to me, so that he may carry me to the house of the dead."

Then the chuubi bird departed.

Later, a red wolf appeared, and the woman was afraid of this animal, so she hid under some bushes, and the red wolf looked about and spoke. "Where are you? My father-in-law said you would be here. Where have you gone?"

Under the bushes, the woman thought. "What was the wolf saying? Where is the chuubi bird?"

After the wolf left, the woman crawled out from under the bushes.

Then, the chuubi bird returned and asked. "What happened? My son-in-law told me that he could not find you." And the woman replied. "I was hiding from a wolf." And the chuubi exclaimed. "That wolf was my son-in-law. I sent him over here to carry you to the house of the dead." And the woman replied. "I could not understand what the wolf was saying, and I did not know that your son-in-law was a wolf." And the chuubi replied. "The wolf is my son-in-law, and it is the role of the fleet red wolf to carry souls to the house of the dead. Now, I know it's better if you forget about going to the house of the dead." The woman protested. "No! Please! Take me to my love."

And so, the chuubi bird could think of no other solution but to lift the woman upon his back and fly her over to the house of the dead.

Then, the woman and the chuubi bird lifted off, and they set forth towards the house of the dead.

As they drew near, the woman could hear the sounds of celebration and drinking.

When they landed, the woman went into the house of the dead.

There, she saw her husband celebrating. She knew, almost, all of the dead, and many of those celebrating were her family.

Then, the woman went up to her husband and exclaimed. "You're here!" Her husband simply remained silent and unresponsive. The woman exclaimed again. "You're here! Aren't you happy to see me?" Her husband did not respond.

Then, the woman went over and sat behind her husband and began to pick the lice out of his hair, and her husband jumped up and beat her.

Now, the woman was angry, and she said to the chuubi bird. "My husband does not love me anymore. Take me back."

Then, the woman climbed upon the back of the chuubi, and they began their flight back home.

When they returned to her village. The chuubi told her. "Now, do you understand why it is better not to go to the house of the dead? There, they live with Yanerataque and are surrounded by beautiful things. They have everything they need, and you have seen it for yourself. Now, you must return and tell all the people of your village of what you have seen."

And so, the woman returned to her village and informed the people.

Then, the woman grew sick and died, and the red wolf came for her and carried her to the house of the dead.

Canto XXXII

The revenge of the Muo

Tesere 11/18/1964

The Muo is a spirit that lives near a person. The Muo is a bothersome annoyance, but it does not want to hurt people. The Muo is one of the three spirits. The others are Yanerataque and Yaneague. These three spirits existed for the Guarasug'we, but they were separate.

Once in the village of the Guarasug'we, there lived a man who was always being visited by the Muo.

When the Muo came to visit the man would invite the Muo. "Come and visit with me and have a drink." And the man and the Muo would visit.

After a while, the man grew tired of the Muo and thought. "I'm going to play a mean trick on the Muo."

During the Muo's next visit, the man asked the Muo. "Would you like to return tomorrow?" "Why?" asked the Muo. And the man replied. "Tomorrow I'll have something special for you." And the Muo exclaimed. "How wonderful! I will return."

After the Muo had left, the man began to plan his mean trick.

Then, he cut off all his hair.

When the Muo returned the following day, the man said. "Look! This is my surprise. I no longer have hair on my head." And the Muo exclaimed! "How lovely you look. Would you cut the hair off my head too?" And the man replied. "Yes, I'll do that for you. Wait here while I go and get a squirrel tooth to cut it with."

Then, the man left and returned with a squirrel's tooth. He called the Muo. "Come over here and sit down on the ground in front of me." And so, the Muo went over and sat down.

Then, the man set up behind him and began to cut. The man did not shave the head of the Muo, he cut through the skin of the Muo's head and scalped him.

Next, he raised the Muo's hairy bloody scalp into the air and declared. "Now, you have no hair upon your head." And the Muo replied. "I will be the most beautiful person in the world."

Now when the Muo saw his hair upon the ground, he skipped away delighted.

Then, the man began to laugh as he thought to himself. "I've scalped the Muo. What a fool I've made of the Muo. The Muo is the most stupid thing in the world."

Afterwards, the man grew afraid of the Muo, and he left his village and settled down far away. He made sure to go far enough away so that when the Muo realized that he had played a mean trick on him that he would be a safe distance away.

For a while, the Muo did not even notice that he had been scalped.

Later the next day, the Muo's head began to hurt.

Then, he touched his head, and he realized that his scalp was gone.

Now, he knew that the man had cut through his skin, and he began to look for the man, and throughout many villages the Muo searched.

At every village, the Muo would laugh and speak. "I've played a funny trick on someone. Is there anyone, here, who has scalped someone?"

The Muo would cover his head, and he would, only, travel by night, for the sun hurt his skinless head.

For a long time, the Muo never found anyone, but just as he was about to give up, he came to the last village.

Here, he sang. "I've scalped someone. Has anybody else played such a funny trick?" And someone said. "Yes, I've scalped someone. Come into my home. I'm glad to meet you." And when the Muo went inside the man's house, they both began to dance. The man did not realize that he was dancing with the Muo.

After a while, the man grew tired and wanted to rest, and he said to the Muo. "I'm going outside to urinate." And the Muo replied. "I'll be right behind you." After the man had finished. The Muo said. "I'll be right there." And as the man was waiting, the Muo picked up a club and crushed the man's skull.

There, the Muo took his revenge. It is a foolish thing to play mean tricks on the Muo.

Canto XXXIII

Kaapoare, The master of the wild beast and the wilderness

Tesere 12/29/1964

Once there was a Guarasu who lost his way while hunting in the wilderness.

There in the wilderness, he remained unable to find his way home. His hair grew very long, and he learned to speak the languages of the animals.

All the animals called him uncle, and he called each animal uncle.

Now there came a time, when he began to think about his family and of his village, but no matter how long he thought, he could not remember the way back to his village.

And so, he asked his animal friends, and they remember how he got to where he was, and they agreed to help him return.

And so, he set out, he came to a wide river that he was unable to cross.

Here, he waited by the river bank. He saw a duck on the river, and he thought. "I'm sure that that duck knows where there is boat."

Then, the duck swam close to him and asked. "Do you need a boat? I can help you get one." And the man replied. "Yes! Uncle I do need a boat." And the duck swam away.

Then, the duck returned siting on a caiman. "This caiman will be your boat." The man was very much afraid of the caiman, but he said nothing. He climbed onto the caiman's back, and they headed out into the river.

Next, the caiman swam out into the middle of the river. And soon, the man and the caiman were passing through mazes of rivers, lakes, and swamps.

All the time, the man said nothing.

Then, the caiman spoke. "Insult me. Tell me I'm stupid, ugly, and rotten. Tell me that I let strong farts. Tell me that I'm a smelly, miserable, horrible, ugly, stupid thing." And the man replied. "How can I say that you are stupid, ugly, and filthy. When you are intelligent, beautiful, friendly, and clean."

Then, another caiman swam by and said to the caiman carrying the man. "Friend let's eat that man." And the caiman replied. "How can we eat our uncle when he has not insulted me?"

Now, the man was filled with fear, and he looked for an escape.

And when the caiman floated near a tree the man grabbed a tree branch and pulled himself up into the tree.

And when he was secure in the tree he yelled at the caiman. "I was afraid of you. You are ugly, stupid, and filthy. And the caiman replied. "I'm going to eat you."

Then, the man jumped out of the tree and ran into the tall trees as fast as he could. And the caiman said to his friend. "Wait for me here in the water."

As the man was running through the trees, he came upon a little bird, and he said to the little bird. "The caiman is after me. Would you help me find my way back to my village?" And the little bird replied. "Yes, I will help you. Take this trail, and you will come to a group of bare headed birds, and they will help you."

And so, the man went down the trail, and the little bird covered over the man's footprints.

When the caiman arrived, he asked the little bird. "Did you see a man come by here?" And the little bird replied. "No, I've not seen any man at all." The caiman looked carefully about, and he found a footprint and he declared. "Here is a man's footprint." The little bird said nothing, for he had missed a footprint.

Then, the caiman continued to pursue the man.

Now, the man came to where the bare headed birds were fishing, and the bare headed birds asked him. "Why are you running away uncle?" And he told them. "A caiman is after me, and he wants to kill and eat me. Could you help me escape?" And they replied. "Yes, we will help you."

Then, one of the bare headed birds swallowed the man.

Now when, the caiman arrived he asked the bareheaded birds. "Has a man came by here." And they replied. "No, no man has passed through here."

Then caiman looked all around, but he could not find a sign of the man. The caiman walked off and slid into the water.

There, he ate a spine fish, and he choked to death because one of the spines got stuck in his gullet.

Then, the bare headed bird spat the man out.

After he was out, he asked the bare headed birds. "Could you help me find my village and my family?" And the birds replied. "We will help you, but you must stay and have dinner with us." Although the man was very hungry, he declined the invitation. "No thank you, I want to get back to my home and family." And the bare headed birds replied. "Okay then don't eat with us, but you must come to our village." And the man asked in surprise. "How! Can I go to your village, for I cannot fly?" And they replied. "We will dress you in feathers."

And so, the bare headed birds dressed the man in feathers, and the man tried to fly, and on his third attempt he lifted off the ground, and the man and the birds came to the village of the bareheaded birds.

It was a large village with many dwellings circling a lagoon. The village had both a chief and a sub chief. The village was open and friendly, and they welcomed the man. "Come into our village as a friend, for we have known you for a long time, for we have watched you wander in the wilderness. How do you like our village? Isn't our village beautiful?" and the man replied. "Yes, indeed your village is beautiful."

Later the village chief said to the man. "I will give you my daughter for you wife if you stay with us." And the man replied. "Your daughter is very special and this is a wonderful gift, but I have a wife and children, and I must get back home." And the chief replied. "I understand, but stay here awhile and rest."

So then, the man stayed in the village of the bare headed birds and relaxed.

And when the birds gathered again, they lifted off taking the man with them. They flew until they came to a lake.

Here, the birds told the man. "Turn yourself around three times." And when the man did as the birds told him, all the feathers fell off, and the man asked the birds. "Will you help me find my way back home?" And the bare headed birds explained. "You must take that path over there. In time you will come to a deer. And from where you meet the deer, you must travel past the house of the toucans. And from there, you go to were the agouti lives. The agouti lives very near your village."

And so, the man started out.

Then, he came up to the deer as it was eating some peanuts. And the deer said to him. "Come and eat some peanuts with me." And the man asked the deer. "Do you know where my family is? Could you help me find them?" And the deer replied. "Yes, I can help you, but you must talk with my cousin in the tall trees." The deer pointed out the trail to the home of his cousin.

And so, the man set out into the tall trees.

When he came to the deer, he said. "Good day uncle can I come into your house and talk to a while?" And the deer replied. "Yes, come in and eat with me." And the man went into the deer's home and said. "I'm very tired, can I rest in your house." And the deer replied. "Yes, you can rest here. You can sleep over there, it will soon be night fall, and we will both rest. If you get cold during the night, go over and warm yourself by the fire, but don't touch me, for if you do, I'll get scared and run away."

And so, the man and the deer of the tall trees went to bed for the night.

During the night the man got cold, and he reached over and touched the deer. The deer sprang to its feet and ran away, ever after that deer are afraid of men and run away.

Early next morning, the man set out for home. He came to the house of the toucans, and found them in a happy mood, they were so playful that they did not notice when he entered their house.

When they finally noticed him, they asked. "Is that you uncle! How is it that you have come to our home?" And he replied. "I was running from the caiman, for he wanted to eat me. The bareheaded birds told me how to find my way home, and the little deer and the deer of the tall trees have helped me. They told me that I would pass by here, so I've come to your house." Then, the toucans said. "We are going to help you, but have some of our flower nectar first." And the man replied. "No thank you. I must return home quickly." And the toucans replied. "We will fly ahead of you and help you find the way."

And so, the toucans put of their most beautiful feathers. They had beautiful green feathers and feathers as blue as the sky. They had red, pink, and purple feathers.

And then, they took to the air, and they flew towards the man's village.

Then, then man set out on the path in the direction that the toucans indicated. Soon he came to the place where the agouti lived.

There, he found the agouti, and the agouti greeted him. "Good day uncle. Come over and have something to eat with me." And the man replied. "I'm not hungry, for I'm in a hurry to return to my village, for I have not seen my family for a long time."

Now, the agouti was insistent, and the man was very hungry, so he went over and ate with the agouti.

Here, the man broke the law of the universe, for anyone who eats the food of an animal will become an animal.

The following day, the man returned home, and his friends and family did not know him. Only the macaw could recognize him, and the macaw said. "Our uncle has returned to us."

Then, his family recognized him. His family tried to change him, but he said to them. "I have eaten the food of the animals, and you can't change me. They continued to insist that he act human, but he did not want to change, so he decided to get sick and die.

His spirit returned to the wilderness.

There, he speaks the languages of the animals, and he can speak the language of man.

Now, he is the master of the animals, and the master of the wilderness. He is the great Kaapoare.

Although the original Spanish document did include a Canto XXXIV, I decided not to translate and present it. The Canto was garbled and incoherent. And it appeared to have been damaged in the translating and printing.

Canto XXXV

Amerahuda the guardian of dogs

Tesere 1/4/1965

And then it came to pass that a hunter went into the tall trees to look for game.

There, he saw a tapir.

Then, he saw three more tapirs. He killed all four animals and began to butcher them.

Then, the hunter was surrounded by a pack of small dogs. He tried to escape, but every time he moved away, the dogs moved in closer.

Now, behind the dogs was an enormous man, and the man began to speak to him in a powerful voice. "Why have you killed four tapirs? One tapir is enough for you and your family. Why do you steal the food from my dogs.?" And the hunter replied. "I was not aware that those tapirs belonged to someone." And the enormous man replied. "Those animals are the prey of my dogs. They belong to Kaapoare the great master of the tall trees."

Now, the man was speechless. And the giant spoke. "You are to have none of the meat from those tapirs, because you have killed more than you needed. Return to your village, and tell the people that they are never to kill more animals than they need."

And so, the man returned to his village, and he said to the people. "I killed four tapirs, and then the giant Amerahuda appeared and took all their meat from me. He commanded me to kill only what I needed, and to tell all the people never to kill more than you need."

Now, the people understood that the hunter had been lucky that the giant only took the meat from him and did not kill him.

Now, the people understand that they must never kill more than they need.

Canto XXXVI

The master of pigs Tadahuda

Tesere 1/6/1965

Once upon a time, a man of our people went into the tall trees to hunt. He spotted a wild pig and shot it. The pig ran away bleeding, and the hunter followed it until he came to an enormous rock deep in the tall trees.

Now, the hunter had never been into this area before, and he was amazed by the great rock formations around him. He walked up to the great rock to touch it.

Then, an enormous man appeared before him and spoke. "Don't be afraid. Let's go into my house."

And so, the hunter went into the house of the enormous man.

There, lived Tadahuda the master of the wild pigs. The hunter looked around in wonder. He saw many things. He saw arrows, chains, and clubs. He saw things that he had lost years ago. Tadahuda said to him. "Go and take a closer look." And the man examined the objects more closely.

Then, Tadahuda said. "Come let's go outside, for I have something that I wish to demonstrate."

Then, they went outside. To where there were pig pens.

In one of the pens there were healthy pigs, and in the other, there were wounded pigs. The hunter looked closer, and he saw the pig that he had wounded. And Tadahuda said to him. "It is not right that these animals should run wild, for they have my mark on them, and I must care for them when they are wounded. Some hunters aim badly and wound these animals, and to those hunters I will send no more pigs. Let this be a lesson to you to never aim poorly or to torture or kill more animals than you need. If you have a small family, you can take two animals, and if you have a large family, you can take four animals." And the hunter replied. "I will try, always, to be more thoughtful."

Then, Tadahuda asked him. "Would you like this feathered headdress?" And the hunter responded. "Yes, I'd like have it very much! It is the most beautiful headdress I've ever seen." And Tadahuda replied. "Let's make a deal." And the hunter replied. "What would you want in exchange for the headdress?" And Tadahuda replied. "I would like your daughter." And the hunter replied. "Okay, it's a deal, now I must return to my village and tell my daughter."

And so, the hunter returned home.

There, he drank strong drink until he very drunk, but he said nothing to his daughter.

Then, he returned to the house of Tadahuda and said. "My daughter agrees to the deal. She, only, wants to spend this day with her mother, and tomorrow I'll bring her to you." And Tadahuda replied. "Very well so it will be. You bring her to me tomorrow." And the hunter asked Tadahuda. "Can I take the headdress home with me?" and Tadahuda gave him the headdress.

Then, the man returned to his village.

There, everyone praised the beautiful feathers and the fine construction of the headdress, but the man never thought to say anything to his daughter.

The following night, the hunter and his daughter became feverish and died. The men of the village looked for the beautiful feathered headdress, but it was gone.

Here, Tadahuda recovered his property. Tadahuda is good to us, but if he is lied to, he becomes angry and takes vengeance. Tadahuda is more powerful than a man.

Canto XXXVII

Kurupi-Vgra (the hairy man creature)

Tesere 1/28/1965

And so, it came to pass those two men were out in the tall trees hunting. Often these two men would hunt together. One of these two hunters were a good hunter, but the other hunter was unsuccessful and had never killed an animal. The good hunter permitted the bad hunter to hunt with him, for the bad hunter was very strong and could carry the game back to the village.

Then one day, the two hunters became separated, and they could not find each other. The bad hunter was very sad and thought. "What will I do now? I can't help this good hunter carry his game home, so he won't share any of the meat with me."

And so, he sat down upon a tree trunk.

Then, he heard a faint sound, and he thought. "Is that my friend calling?" He began traveling in the direction from where the sound was coming from. He came to a lagoon, and out in the lagoon, he saw a strange thing. It had the appearance of a man, but it was completely covered with long hairs.

Now, the man wanted to run away, but the creature called out. "Don't leave me! A great anaconda has trapped me. Come and help me."

The man stepped back to catch his breath, for he was scared senseless.

Once he collected himself, he replied. "How can I help you?" And the creature replied. "Take that little stick of wood that is over there in that tree. Use that stick of wood to tap the water around me, but tap gently, for if you tap to hard, it will kill me."

And so, the man went and got the stick and tapped the water around the hairy man. The anaconda's body fell off the hairy man, the hairy man escaped.

After they were away from the lagoon, the creature said. "I'm grateful to you. My name is Kurupi-Vgra, and I'm going to reward you. I know that you are a bad hunter, but I'm going to help you become a good hunter. And all the hunters in your village will respect you." And the man replied. "I understand your gratitude, but I don't understand hunting." And the creature replied. "It's easy just tale that hardwood stick that you used to free me, and when you see an animal tap the stick in the direction of the animal, and the animal will fall down dead. Strike lightly and never kills more animals than you can use. When you're done, always return the stick to the tree where you first found it, the stick will always be where you left it. Don't tell anyone about the stick, or you will lose it."

Then, the hairy man creature vanished.

Now, the bad hunter took the hardwood stick, and as he walked through the tall trees.

Then, he saw a tapir, and he taped the stick in the direction of the tapir, and it fell to the ground.

Then, he saw a wild pig, and he tapped the stick towards the pig, and it fell down.

Then, he carried all the meat home.

There, the people were very surprised, for this hunter had never brought home meat before.

And so, the hunter continued to bring home meat, and he became the most respected hunter in the village, and he keep the secret of the stick.

Every day he would go out hunting, and when he was done, he returned the stick to its place in the tree, and every morning the stick would be where he had left it.

Then one day, a young man said to him. "I'm a bad hunter, could I go hunting with you, and help you carry the game home?"

Now, the man did not know what to say, for it would not be right to say no, yet he wanted to guard his secret.

Then man allowed the young man to go hunting with him, and before they came to where the killing stick was stored, the man had given away all the secrets.

And when they came to the tree where the stick was kept, and it was gone.

The man never found the killing stick. Kurupi-Vgra will help hunters, and lend them his weapons, and he is our friend.

Canto XXXVIII

Ivitapoare (The angel of the mountain)

Hapik'wa 11/15/1964

Once upon a time, a Guarasu and his family went to live in the tall trees, and while they were out hunting, a young boy became separated from his family.

As the boy was wandering about, he came to an enormous rock.

Here, Ivitapoare the beautiful angel of the mountains appeared in front of him.

Then, Ivitapoare said. "Come into my house." And the boy and Ivitapoare went inside the great rock.

There, the boy stayed with Ivitapoare and the spirit's husband.

Then one day, the husband of Ivitapoare said. "The boy's parents are missing him, and they are constantly crying. Let the boy return to his parents and comfort them." Ivitapoare turned and asked the boy. "Do you want to return to your parents?" And the boy replied, "No, I wish to stay here with you. I'm happy here, and I do not wish to return to my village. I love you, and I could never leave you." And Ivitapoare replied. "Go and tell your parents that from now on you will be living with me. Tell them that all is beautiful here, and you are very happy. Then, return to me."

And so, the boy returned to his village.

There, his parents very happy to see him, but they could see that the boy had changed. All the people in his village commented. "This boy has changed. He is different." And the boy told everyone. "I'm going to return to the great rock and to the angel." And his parents replied. "Will you not stay with us, for it is very good here?" And the boy answered them. "It is much more beautiful there than it is here. The house of the angel is where I want to live. There, I have all I need, and I've never been so happy."

Then his parents were no longer worried, and the boy returned to Ivitapoare.

There, his lives inside the great rock by a beautiful lake. He never grows old, and he always young and fair. He may someday become an angel appear before young men.

Canto XXXIX

The angel of the mountains takes a man away

Tesere 2/3/1965

Once upon a time, a party of men were out hunting.

After they had killed enough animals and prepared the meat, they separated and went into the tall trees to look for honey.

Out in the tall trees, one of the men came upon an unusual rock. The rock was different than any other rock he had seen before.

And so, he stopped to look.

Then, a very beautiful angel appeared. The angel had long flowing hair and smooth iridescent skin. This was Ivitapoare.

Then, Ivitapoare said to him. "Come into my house."

And so, the hunter wen into the house in the great rock.

There, he saw many beautiful and unique things.

Here, the angel said to the man. "Stay with me and be my lover, for I will not let you return to your village." And the hunter replied. "I will be glad to stay with you, but let me return to my village for a day to tell my family that I going to live with you from now on." And the angel of the mountains replied. "You may return for two days, and show these precious jewels to your family."

The next day, the hunter returned home.

There, he told his family of his experience with Ivitapoare, and he showed them the jewels, but he did not return to Ivitapoare.

Then, the man became very sick, and soon he died, and the following night Ivitapoare returned and carried the man and the jewels away.

Now, the man lives with Ivitapoare.

Canto XL

Suvipoare the angel of the plains carries off a boy

Jeru'as 2/3/1965

And so, it came to pass that the mother of the boy Suvi sent her son out upon the plains.

There, he went about collecting fruit, and when the boy did not return, the people of the village knew that Suvipoare had carried him away.

Then, the father of Suvi asked the village shaman. "Will you help me find my son?" The shaman replied. "Yes, I will search for your son." The shaman went out into the plains and asked Suvipoare. "Do you have the boy Suvi with you? Can I speak with him?" Suvipoare replied. "The boy is with me, and you can speak with him"

Here, Suvi came out and said to the shaman. "Tell my parents that I'm very happy here. Tell them not to be sad, for here everything is beautiful, and here no one grows old or gets sick or dies."

And so, the shaman returned to the village and said to the family of Suvi. "Your son is with the angel Suvipoare, and he very happy." The family was very happy, for they knew their son was safe.

Now, Suvi lives with Suvipoare, and he always remains young and beautiful. Our Shaman often speaks with Suvipoare and Suvi.

Cantos of the ways of humans and animals

Canto XLI

The Woman who was really a man.

Tesere 11/4/1964

Once upon a time, a brother and sister lived together. Their parents were gone, but they continued to stay together. The sister was ready for marriage, but she did not want a man, and she would often say. "What would I do with a husband? I want to stay here and live with my brother." Her brother allowed her to live with him, but he said to her. "You can stay in this house with me, but I'm not going to take care of you. You will need to hunt and fish for yourself."

Then, the brother gave his sister a bow and arrows told her how to point and shoot.

Now, the young woman soon learned to hunt and fish better than any of the men. She could always bring back strong healthy meat for the villagers.

Then, the people of the village started saying. "That woman is really a man, for that person is a great hunter. We must always think of that person as a man."

And so, it came to pass that a man from another village came to the village of the woman who was really a man.

There, he joined with the men to go hunting.

Then, he saw the woman who was really a man, and he declared. "Why is this woman hunting with us men? Do the women hunt with the men here?" The hunters replied. "We do not call that person a woman, for that person has the strength and courage of a man."

Now when the hunters returned to their village, the visitor was unable to forget about the woman who was really a man. He went back to his village, but he never stopped thinking about the woman who was really a man.

Then, the man returned to the village of the woman who was really a man.

There, he asked the brother of the woman who was really a man. "Could your sister come hunting with me, for I'm not familiar with this area." Her brother replied. "I will tell my brother who once was my sister to help you."

And so, the visitor from another village and the man who once was a woman went into the tall trees to hunt.

There, they killed butchered their kill.

Then, the woman who was really a man over to the river to wash.

There, the man saw that the woman who was really a man was developed as a woman. The woman who was really a man had pubic hair even though she had never had sex with a man.

Now, it was getting dark and to late to return to the village. They constructed a small shelter, and they laid down together for the night.

Here, the man drew closer to the woman who was really a man.

Then, he pulled her pubic hair and penetrated her.

The following day, the couple returned to the village. He told the villagers about everything.

Now, the woman who was really a man belonged to the visitor, and they returned to his village.

There, the woman who was really a man died. It was not a good thing, for her to be with that man.

Canto XLII

The friends

Tesere 3/12/1964

It happened here in a village of our people that there were two friends who would always go hunting together. For every hunting trip they would each pack their supply of manioc flour to sustain them during the hunt.

On the first night of the hunt, they both ate from the provisions of one of the hunters.

The next morning, they both ate again from the provisions of the same hunter.

And so, they continued to each eat the provisions of the same hunter.

And when that hunter whose provisions were feeding both of them ran out of manioc flour he asked. "We have eaten all of my manioc flour. Now, can we eat your manioc flour?" And his partner replied. "No, I want all of my manioc flour for myself."

And then, his partner took a stick and poked out his eyes.

There, he left his partner blind and alone. He paid no attention to his pleas for help and returned to his village.

Now, the blind man stumbled about until he came to a tree. He climbed up into the tree and sat in its branches thinking. "What will I do? I'm surely going to die."

Then, he heard the sound of shamans talking, and they were getting closer.

Here, he could understand what they were saying, and he listened as one of them spoke. "There is a village in which the people have no water. There, the people don't understand that if they dig below the rock, they will have enough water." And then, another shaman spoke. "There is a village in which there is no day light. There, the people don't under-stand that the blue jaguar will not let the sun come out." Then, the third shaman spoke. "There is a village where the chief is blind. No one there knows that the leaves of the tree below where he is sitting could cure his blindness. If someone would tell the chief that if he would only rub his eyes with the leaves of that tree, he could cure his blindness, and the chief would reward him by giving him his beautiful daughter."

Now, the blind man listened to everything that the shamans were saying.

Then, he took some leaves and rubbed them over his eyes and he could see!

Here, he gathered some leaves of that tree and put them into a sack, and he set out through the tall trees to find the village that had no water.

And when he came to that village, the people said to him. "Here, we have no water. Could you help us find water?" And the man who had been blind replied. "To find water you must dig beneath the great rock in the center of your village."

And so, the people dug beneath the great rock and they found a great flow of pure water, and they rejoiced, and they rewarded the man with many beautiful gifts.

Then, the man set out to find the village that had no daylight.

When he found it the people there said to him "We do not have any day-light, so we have to live in constant darkness. Could you help us find the sun?" And the man replied. "I can help you to find daylight."

And so, the man went to chase away the blue jaguar. He chased away the great cat, and the sun came out as soon as the blue jaguar let go of the sun.

Here, the people were very happy, and they rewarded the man with many fine gifts.

Then, the man set out to find the village where the chief was blind. He found the village deep in the tall trees. And he found its chief, and the chief said. "I have lost my sight. Could you help me to see again?" And the man replied. "Yes, I can help you."

There, he took some leaves from out of his sack and rubbed them over the chief's eyes, and he regained his sight.

Now, the chief said. "I'll reward you with my beautiful daughter." And the man was delighted.

Then, the man returned with his new wife to his village.

There, everyone was surprised to see him. He shared all the fine gifts that had been given to him by the grateful villagers of the villages that he had helped. He was named chief of his village.

Then, he had the man who blinded him killed.

Canto XLIII

The castigated man

Tesere 11/12/1964

Once upon a time, the hunters were out far away from their village.

Here, they needed to set up a base camp so that they could return at night and find shelter.

And so, they set up small hunting shelters.

Then, they appointed a hunter to stay at base camp and care for it, and they went out into the tall trees to hunt.

Here, the man that they left alone to care for base camp became very bored, for he was just sitting and waiting. He could not think of anything to do.

Then, he saw a toad and he thought. "If that toad is a female, I could have sex." And he asked the toad. "Are you a female?" And the toad replied. "Yes, I'm a female." And the man said. "Come over here." The toad came over, and the man put his penis in, but when he wanted to take his penis out of the toad's vagina, the toad said. "Leave it in, for it is very pleasant!"

Next, the toad hopped away with the man's penis still stuck inside of her vagina.

Then, the toad hopped up into a tree, and the penis stretched out, and the toad hopped around the tree, and the penis stretched out further and further.

When, the penis finally slipped out of the toad, it had stretched out so far that it wrapped around its owner several times.

When the hunters returned, they laughed at the man, and they spoke. "This is what happens when someone has to wait alone for several days."

And so, the hunters returned to their village, and the man who put his penis in a toad had to carry his penis back to the village in a basket.

And when he returned home, his woman wanted nothing to do with him.

And during the night he wanted a woman, so he sent the penis out to search.

Now, because women like to sleep with their legs apart, the penis quietly entered many women, but when they awoke the next morning, their vaginas would be wet, and they could tell that a penis had found them.

Now, the village chief was always watchful.

And one night, he watched as the penis went out of the house to search.

Then, he took a sharp shell and cut off the penis, and the man bled to death.

Afterwards, the Yanerataque soul of the man haunts the earth, and in the night time he comes to the women while they are sleeping, and they awake with wet vaginas.

Canto XLIV

The mother -in-law

Sawu'I 1/18/1964

Once there was an old woman who was trying to kill her son-in-law.

Every time she wanted to fart, she would run over to him and direct her ass towards him and fart directly in his face.

Now, her son-in-law was becoming very weak from her farts.

Then one day his friend said to him. "If you don't want to die, you must kill your farting mother-in-law."

Then, they decided to kill the evil old woman. They found some poison, and put it on the widened tip of an arrow.

When the old woman came over and turned her ass towards her son-in-law, he drove the arrow up her anus and killed her.

There, the arrow's wide tip prevented the blood from running out of her anus, and they broke off the arrow while it was still inside the old woman so that it was not visible.

Then, they turned the old woman on her back, and cried out to her daughter. "Your poor dear mother is dead."

Now, everyone was sad, and they all began to cry.

Then, they buried the old woman, and her daughter never suspected anything, and the son-in-law lived in peace. Nothing more came of it.

Canto XLV

The Glutton

Tesere 1/18/1965

And so, it happened that a man of our people went into the tall trees to hunt.

There, he found a tapir sleeping. He did not bother to kill the animal with an arrow. He just stuck his arm up the tapir's anus and attempted to pull out its succulent liver.

Then, the tapir awoke, and tightened its anus around the man's arm and bolted away with the man's arm held firmly in its anus.

When the man did not return to his village during the night, the hunters went out to look for him.

The next morning, they could not see a sign of him.

Then, they found the tracks of a tapir with a man's tracks behind them. They followed the double set of tracks until they came to a salt lick.

There, they saw the tapir, and the man's arm was still in it.

Here, the men began to laugh, and the man begged them to kill the tapir and free him, the hunters killed the tapir and set the man free, but they laughed at him and teased him for being so foolish and impatient.

Canto XLVI

The daughter of the chief

Tesere 10/12/1964

Once upon a time a very beautiful young woman lived among our people. She was the daughter of the chief, and she was unmarried.

Then one day, she pointed to a man and said to her father. "That man has made me pregnant." The chief confronted the man. "You have left my daughter pregnant. Now, let's see if you can work as well." The man protested. "No! I did not make your daughter pregnant." And the chief replied. "My daughter says that you did, and she should know." Again, the man protested. "It is not for certain that I made her pregnant!" The chief did not believe him, and he said to the man. "Come to my field early tomorrow morning and harvest twenty acres of corn. If you are not done by night time, I will kill you."

And so, the man went over to the chief's field just as the sun was rising and started working.

He worked without stopping, but his progress was very slow, and by the afternoon he knew that he could never finish.

Then, he sat down in the field and said to himself. "I'm unable to complete this task. Now, the chief will kill me."

Then, a small red ant appeared, and it said to him. "What makes you so sad?" And the man replied. "The daughter of my chief claims that I made her pregnant, but that is not for sure. He did not listen to me, and he commanded me to harvest twenty acres of corn as punishment, and I'm unable to complete the task, and he is going to kill me." And the small red ant replied. "If that is all you need, we can help you."

Then, the small red ant left and returned with an army of red ants. The ants worked steadily and quickly, and after an hour all of the corn field was harvested.

Now, the task was completed, and the sun was still high in the sky. The man gave a grain of corn to every red ant that had helped with the harvest and returned to his village.

There, he told his chief. "I'm done with the harvest of your corn." His chief did not believe him, and he went out to see for himself. He saw all the corn neatly piled up, and he was amazed.

Here, the chief thought for a moment. "I must assign him an absolutely impossible task, so I can kill him when he fails."

Then, the chief said to the man. "Go and find the tapir of seven colors, and if you do not find it before sunset, I will kill you!"

Now, the man was again saddened, and he thought. "How can I find a tapir of seven colors, for they are very rare?"

Then, he went into the tall trees, he looked for a tapir of seven colors, but he found nothing. He sat down beside a tree in despair.

Then, a red wolf came up to him and spoke. "Friend why are you so sad?" And the man replied. "The chief of my village demands that I find a rare tapir of seven colors before sunset. If I do not complete this impossible task, he will kill me." And the red wolf replied. "If this is all you need, I can help you. Come I will take you to where you can find a tapir of seven colors."

And so, the man climbed upon the back of the red wolf, and they set forth into the tall trees.

Then, they found a tapir of seven colors, and the man killed and skinned it. He gave the meat to the red wolf and carried the hide of the tapir back to his village.

There, he showed his chief the hide of the tapir, and his chief said. "You have harvested a field of twenty acres of corn in one day, and you have found a tapir of seven colors. Now, you can have my daughter for you have clearly shown that you can work."

Then, the man went to the house of the chief's daughter. And he called out. "Untie the covering from your door so that I can enter." He received no answer. Again, he called out. "Untie the covering from your door so that I can enter." Again, there was no answer.

Then, a chuubi bird landed upon a nearby tree. And the chuubi said to the man. "Come I will carry you up to where you can enter her house."

Then, the man went over to the chuubi, and the great raptor picked him up and placed him on the roof of her house.

Then, the man climbed through a hole in the roof and found the chief's daughter.

There, he said to her. "Why did you tell your father that I made you pregnant? And she replied, "I don't know why I said this to him." She paused for a moment and then continued. "I told him this and said no more, but when I saw that my father had put you to task, I was afraid for you, and I did not want to tell him that I had lied, for surely he would have killed me."

Now, the chuubi bird circled up into the sky, and he flew over the tall trees until he came to the house of the souls of children.

There, he picked up a child's soul and carried it back to the daughter of the chief. And the chuubi said to her. "Take this child's soul within you and don't be afraid."

And so, the man and the daughter of the chief lived together in peace, and she was a good wife and caused no trouble.

Canto XLVII

The sickly sister

Tesere 12/29/1964

Once upon a time there were two brothers who lived with their sister.

Then one day, the sister became very weak, and she was not strong enough to travel with her brothers.

And when the time came for the village to relocate, the woman was not able to walk, so they prepared a stretcher and put her on it.

Then, they started out with each brother taking turns dragging the stretcher.

When they came to where they were going to camp, the brothers prepared a shelter of leaves for their sister, and they said to her. "Rest here a while. We are going into the tall trees to hunt."

Then, the brothers went into the tall trees.

They returned much later, and when they went to look in on their sister, they saw that she had not gotten up from the stretcher in all the time that they had been gone. They lifted her out of the stretcher and found that she had soiled herself.

Now, the brothers realized that their sister was seriously ill and the oldest brother said. "Our dear sister is going to die if she doesn't have sex. One of us must have sex with her. We can decide who will have sex with her by a contest. We will both shoot an arrow, and the one whose arrow goes the farther does not have to have sex with our sister."

And so, they shot their arrows.

Then, the brother whose arrow fell short had sex with his sister that night.

When they returned from hunting the following day, the sister appeared stronger, and again her brother had sex with his sister that night.

Now, the brothers began looking for an unrelated man to have sex with their sister, but their sister became sick again and died.

Here, the brothers were trying to save their sister, but their sister died anyway. Their sister needed sex, but when a brother and sister have sex one of them must die.

Canto XLVIII

The death of the evil mother-in-law

Tesere 12/2/1964

Once there was a man who lived with a cruel mother-in-law.

Every day he went out hunting because his mother-in-law wanted fatty meat to eat. If he killed an animal that did not have enough fat, he was afraid to bring it back to her. And if he came back with no meat, he would have to sleep outside.

Now, he was always hunting and never finding an opportunity to rest. This continued until the man was very weak and sickly.

Then one day, a friend said to him. "You are going to die, if you don't kill you mother-in-law." And the man asked. "How can I kill her?" And his friend explained. "You must go over to the water and watch for ripples and cast your net to catch the poison yakunauhu fish cut out some of the fat from its stomach and give it to your mother-in-law to eat."

And so, the man went fishing, and he caught a yakunauhu fish. He cut out the fat from its stomach and gave it to his mother-in-law."

Here, his mother-in-law retorted. "Why have you brought me so little fat? Go back and bring me more." And the man left.

Then, the nagging old woman ate every bit of the fat from the yakunauhu fish, and soon she felt a pain in her stomach, and in a little while she died.

Now, the man's wife cried over her mother, and the man cried too.

And so, the man had his revenge, and he settled down to a good meal and later rested.

Canto XLXIX

The old woman

Tesere 1/2/1965

Now it came to pass, that there was an old woman living in a village of our people. And living with her was a young man who she had adopted and raised.

Perhaps, she expected the boy to become her husband, or maybe she expected the young man would wait until she was dead and then look for a wife.

However, things took their own course.

Then one day, while the old woman and the young man were sleeping a man entered their cottage. This man had been drinking and celebrating, and he wanted the old woman to drink some corn beer with him. He spoke. "Come and celebrate with me." The old woman and the man began to drink and celebrate.

Then, their laughter woke up the young man, and he heard the old woman say to the man. "Come and lay down with me."

Next, he could hear their groans of pleasure, and he heard the old woman say. "Don't go now leave your hard penis in me, for it feels so good."

The following day, the young man told his friend about what the old woman and that man had done. And his friend replied. "That old woman is no good. You must leave her and go to another village."

And so, the young man abandoned the old woman. He went to another village and married a young woman.

Then, the old woman was all alone. Nobody would help her tend her garden, and nobody would hunt for her. The people of her village ridiculed her. "Your young man is gone. He has abandoned you." She was filled with shame.

Canto L

The old woman's punishment

Hapik'wa 1/2/1965

Once this happened during a celebration in our village.

Here, an old woman got very drunk on corn beer, and when her daughter confronted her and spoke. "Come it's time to go home, for you are very drunk." She refused to leave.

Then, the old woman began to sing. "I want a man. I want his penis in my vagina. I want him to leave it in me for a long lovely time." The old woman sang this song over and over.

Now, her daughter demanded. "Come it's time to go, for you are too old." And the old woman replied. "No! I want to stay here." And she continued to sing. "I want a man. I want his penis in my vagina…"

Again, her daughter demanded. "Come it's time to go, for you are too old." And the old woman replied. "No! I want to stay here." And she continued to sing. "I want a man…"

Then, her daughter took a club and smashed her head.

Here, the daughter did what was right.

Canto LI

The unfaithful wife

Tesere 1/28/1965

And so, it came to pass that in our village there lived a married woman.

Now, the woman wanted nothing to do with her husband, for she had another man. Her husband did not know anything about it. And when he wanted sex, she would say. "Go away."

Now, her husband thought. "Surely she must have a lover, and I will find out right away."

Then, he told his wife. "I'm going hunting, and I will return tomorrow morning."

Now, the man did not go hunting, but he hid himself inside a well, and when his wife came to wash herself, he could see that someone had been pulling on her pubic hair. And he thought. "She has a lover, for she is losing pubic hair."

The next evening, the man appeared before his wife and spoke. "I've killed three wild pigs out in the tall trees, and I need your help to prepare the meat."

And so, the man and his wife went into the tall trees.

Here, the woman collected firewood, and the man built a fire.

Then, the man grabbed his wife and tied her up with a vine.

Next, he threw her into fire. She screamed! "Why are you killing me?" And he replied. "You have a lover, and now you must die."

After his wife was dead and cooked, the man pulled her out of the fire, and with a sharp shell, he cut out her sexual organs, and wrapped them up in a leaf.

Then, he returned to his village.

Here, he gave package to his mother-in-law and said to her. "I've brought you some flavorful meat." And the old woman ate it with pleasure. She asked. "What kind of meat was that?" And the man replied. "It was the sexual organs of your daughter. She betrayed me, and you knew about it, and you let her act that way?"

Then, the old woman began to cry, but she was guilty. She should have stopped her daughter.

Canto LII

The indolent son-in-law

Tesere 12/6/1965

Once upon a time in a village of our people there lived a man who wanted to marry.

There, he told his prospective mother-in-law. "I'm going into the tall trees to hunt."

Then, the man went into the tall trees, but he did not hunt. He sat on the bank of a river and waited and watched the river.

Then, he saw a tortoise, and he took an arrow and pushed it into the anus of the tortoise until it pierced its intestine.

After the arrow was very bloody, he pulled it out and broke off the point.

That evening, the man returned to his village, and said to his prospective mother-in-law. "I've killed two caimans, but I was not able to carry them back. Here look at the broken bloodied arrow I used."

Then, the old woman sent two men out into the tall trees to recover the game, and when they came to the place where the man said that he had left the game.

Here, they found a tortoise with a bleeding anus, and they surmised that the man had not hunted any game.

And they proclaimed. "This man is a liar, and he is indolent. Come let's go find some meat."

Then, they went into the swamps and killed a caiman, and they carried it back to the village.

There, they told the old woman. "Your prospective son-in-law lied. He did not hunt or kill anything. He rammed an arrow into the intestines of a tortoise, and that is how the arrow became bloodied."

Then, the old woman called her prospective son-in-law over and said to him. "You are not a man or a hunter. You are a liar. I will not give my daughter to you."

And so, the man lost the woman he wanted, and the woman married one of the hunters.

Canto LIII

The man who treated men as women

Tesere 11/27/1964

Once there lived among our people an older man who had no woman.

Now, he liked the company of men, and he was very popular with young men, for he was a very good hunter.

When he was out hunting with a young man, he would say. "Come over here and bend over. I want to put my penis in your anus." Or he would say. "Put your penis in my little hole."

Then one day, the man and a youth went out hunting.

After they had sex, they returned to the village.

There, the youth told the man's son-in-law what had happened. The son-in-law declared. "This should not be happening. The next time you and my father-in-law go out into the tall trees to hunt, I'm going to follow and see for myself what is going on."

And so, the man and the youth returned to the tall trees, and his son-in-law followed them.

There, he watched as they had sex.

Then, the son-in-law returned to the village.

Here, he told his wife. "Your father has sex with young men." And his wife replied. "If that's what he likes to do, It's fine with me. Let it alone."

Then, he went to his mother-in-law and declared. "Do you know that the father of your daughter has sex with young men out in the trees." The old woman did not answer. And he shouted at her. "He treats men like women."

Then, the old woman took a club and smashed in his head, for he had no right to interfere in the affairs of his father-in-law.

Canto LIV

The rights of a man over his woman

Hapik'wa 2/2/1965

And so, it came to pass that a man returned to his house with his woman.

There, the man said. "Let's have sex." And she replied. "No not now can't you see that I'm carrying a load? And I don't want to."

Later, they had something to eat, and the man was no longer hungry, but the woman wanted to eat more.

Again, the man said. "Let's have sex." She replied. "No! I can't. Can't you see that I'm still hungry? I don't want to."

After, the woman had eaten even more, the man repeated. "Let's have sex." She replied. "No! I don't want to."

Much later, company came and the man said again. "Let's have sex." And she replied. "No! I don't want to, for we have company.

Always, this happened. The woman had some excuse.

Finally, the man took a club and killed her.

Now, this was a good thing to do.

Canto LV

The faithful wife

Tarekuve 1/27/1965

And so, it came to pass those two men wanted to know if their wives were having sex with other men when they were away from their village.

Then, they thought of a way to find out.

And so, they told their wives. "We are going out to hunt, and we will return early tomorrow."

Then, they hid themselves near their village, and during the night they disguised themselves by putting on different clothes and changing their voices.

Then, they went up to the hammocks of their wives. One of the women refused the strange man, but the other let the stranger into her hammock.

Now, the men knew what was happening, and the woman who gave consent was very much afraid, for she knew her husband had tested her.

Then, the husband of the woman who gave consent took a bamboo spear and killed his wife, and the other man praised his faithful wife.

Canto LVI

The rubber tree tapers

Tesere 1/12/1965

Now it came to pass that a young man wanted to marry the daughter of a rubber tree tapper.

And so, he went to his prospective father-in-law and asked him. "Can I have your daughter for my wife?" And his prospective father-in-law replied. "Yes, you can marry her, if you know how to work, but first you must demonstrate to me that you can work." And the young man asked. "How can I demonstrate this to you?" And the old rubber tree taper replied. "Meet me tomorrow morning in front of my rubber trees."

Early next morning, the young man and his prospective father-in-law met in front of the old man's rubber trees.

There, the old man said. "I have two hundred rubber trees. Go and collect the sap from all two hundred, and I you are done before noon, you can have my daughter."

Then, the young man started to work. He went to the platforms of each of the trees and scratched them so that the sap would run. He collected the sap from the first group of trees and proceeded.

Although, he worked without stopping until the sun was high, he was far from being done.

He continued on until nightfall, and he collected the sap from the last tree. He knew that he had failed, for he had not completed the task before the sun was high.

And so, the young man returned to the house of the rubber tree tapper and spoke. "I was not able to finish in time." The rubber tree tapper replied. "Yes, I could see that you couldn't do it. What good is it for you to have my daughter if you can't take care of her? Go away for now but come back after a while."

Now, the young man had learned to work, and later he married the daughter of the rubber tree tapper.

Canto LVII

The monkeys

Tesere 1/2/1965

And so, it came to pass that once there was a man who did not want to have much to do with others.

And so, the man would go hunting alone in the tall trees all the time. His friends told him. "Don't go hunting alone, for if something would happen to you there, and you would need help there would be no one to help you." The man paid no attention to their advice, and he went out into the tall trees hunting.

There, he saw a group of monkeys, and he shot an arrow into one of them. The other monkeys pulled the arrow out and tried to stop the bleeding, but the wounded monkey fell out of the tree dead.

Then, the rest of the monkeys attacked the man and killed him.

When the man did not return that evening, the men of the village went out to look for him. They found him covered with bites, and they understood what had happened.

Our people kill all monkeys, for they are our enemies. We kill them, but rarely do we eat their flesh, for it has no fat, and if you eat their skinny arms, it will make your arms skinny and weak like a monkey.

Canto LVIII

The man who was afraid

Tesere 2/2/1965

And so, it came to pass that there was a man and a woman who lived in our village, and they had many children.

Then, one night when the moon was full, the man went out to hunt, for he could see by the moonlight.

And upon his return, he watched as two jaguars went into his house.

Here, the man was filled with fear and climbed a tree.

Inside his house, the jaguars killed his wife and children.

Then, the jaguars went after the man. They surrounded the tree, but the man shot them dead.

Now, the man had killed the jaguars that killed his family, but he was a bad husband and father, for he had not defended his family.

And so, the people of the village expelled him.

Canto LIX

The ant

Yeruv'sa 2/4/1965

Although the ubiquitous ant is found almost everywhere on earth, they are of particular importance to the understanding of tropical forest cultures, for their numbers are very great and their societies very elaborate. And most importantly, they impact human culture through their disruption of agriculture.

In the time before our time, the ant was a woman. She would never tend her own garden but would go into the gardens of others and steal.

Then one day, Yaneramai appeared.

He went over to the ant woman to see what the ant woman was doing.

Here, the ant woman covered up what she had stolen.

And when, Yaneramai asked her. "What have you got in your basket?" And the ant woman replied. "My basket is filled with manioc from my garden."

Then, Yaneramai went up to the ant woman and said. "The strap on your basket is loose. I'll help you tighten it."

When the ant woman drew closer, and Yaneramai pulled on the strap until he stretched out the woman's abdomen.

Now the woman had the shape of an ant, and the ant woman robs our gardens.

Canto LX

The man who twice took the same woman

Tesere 1/30/1965

And so, it came to pass that a certain young man wanted to marry the daughter of an old man.

Here, the old man did not want his daughter to marry this young man and refused to give his permission.

Then, the young man asked his friend. "How can I marry that young woman when her father won't give his permission?" And his friend replied. "You must go to where that young woman takes a bath, and hide yourself nearby, and when she takes off her skirt, you must take the skirt and hide it. And when she is finished bathing and wants to get dressed, you must make her promise you marry you before you give her back her skirt."

And so, the young man set out to do what his friend advised him to do. He went to the lagoon, and hid himself.

When the maiden arrived, she took off her skirt and went into the water to bathe.

Then, he stole her skirt.

When the maiden came out of the water, she said to him. "Give me back my skirt." And he replied. "I'll only give you back your skirt if you agree to marry me."

Now, the young woman complained, but final she said. "Okay I'll be you wife."

Then, they had sex.

Then, the man went to talk to her father and spoke. "Your daughter is now my woman, for I have pulled her pubic hair. Will you give us permission to marry?" And he replied. "I'll give you permission to marry when you have demonstrated your ability to work. You must complete three tasks, and after those tasks are completed, you can have my daughter."

Now, the old man secretly thinking. "I'm going to kill him. I'll kill him somehow."

Then, the old man said to the suitor of his daughter. "Go now into the tall trees and look for enough firewood to fill two sheds."

And so, the young man began to gather firewood, but there was a great deal left to do when his young woman appeared.

Then, he said to her. "Tell your father that I'm looking for firewood." And she replied. "I already know that just sit down and rest while I pick the lice out of your hair."

Then the young man sat down, and he fell asleep.

When he awoke, the two sheds were full of firewood. And the young woman said. "Go and tell my father that you have completed the task."

And so, the young man went and said to her father. "The sheds are full."

Now, the old man was very surprised, but he thought. "I want to kill and eat him. I will give him an even more impossible task."

Then, the old man said. "Go into my fields and gather up all the rocks. You must complete this task before the sun is high."

And so, the young man went out into the fields to gather up all the rocks.

There, the young woman appeared, and he said to her. "Your father wants me to gather up all the rocks in his fields." And she replied. "Yes, I know that just sit down and rest while I pick the lice out of your hair." He sat down beside her, and she picked the lice out of his hair.

When he awoke, all of the rocks were piled neatly together, and the young woman said. "Go and tell my father that the task is complete."

And so, the young man told her father. "All of the rocks in your fields are neatly piled up."

Now the old man was very surprised, and he went out into his fields to investigate.

And when he saw that the task was complete, he thought. "I'll have a more impossible job for him, and he will fail, and I will kill and eat him."

Here, the old man said. "Go and build a bridge across the waters."

And so, the young man went to the edge of the waters.

Then, the young woman appeared.

There, he said to her. "Your father wants me to build a bridge across the waters." And she replied. "Yes, I know that now sit down while I pick the lice from your hair."

And when he awoke, he saw that the bridge was built.

And he went to the old man and told him. And the old man replied. "Tomorrow you will have my daughter."

Then, the young man went away, And the old man said to his daughter. "Tomorrow we will kill and eat him."

Then, the young woman went to find her young man, and when she found him, she said. "My father wants to kill and eat you. We must get away from here and go out into the tall trees, and we must search for the tapir of seven colors and return it to my father."

There, in the tall trees the young man searched for the tapir of seven colors, but he could not find it. He told the young woman. "I could not find the tapir if seven colors." She replied. "Wait here. I will bring it to you."

Then, the young woman went into the tall trees to look. She returned riding the tapir of seven colors.

There, the young man climbed upon the back of this animal, and the couple rode away towards the south.

Now, the young woman's father was resting in his hammock thinking that his daughter was still next to him listening to him, but his daughter had taken the saliva that talks out of her throat and placed it in a shell.

There, he was saying to his daughter. "Tomorrow we will kill that young man and eat him." And the saliva responded. "Yes father, we will kill and eat him tomorrow."

Here, the old man talked to the saliva in the shell the entire night, but in the morning the saliva did not respond, and he went over to investigate, and he discovered that he had been tricked.

Then, he set out in pursuit. He found the trail of the tapir, and he understood that the lovers had ridden away.

Here, the daughter knew that her father was after them, so she disguised the young man as an old beggar and changed herself into a great tree.

When the old man caught up, he asked the old beggar. "Has a tapir of seven colors passed this way?" And the old beggar responded. "What are you talking about? A tapir of seven colors, I've never seen such a thing!" The old man did not recognize the young man in disguise, and he returned to the village.

Then, the tree changed back into a young woman and the old beggar into the young man, and they proceeded until they came to a village.

Here, the young man said. "This is where my parents live. Let's go into the village and greet them." And the young woman responded. "No, I must not go into your village. You must go alone into your village and greet your parents, but don't embrace them, for if you do, you will lose me."

And so, the young man went into his village. He found his parents and embraced them.

Then, he settled down to live with his parents and forgot about the young woman.

Later, the young woman went into the village, but the young man did not recognize her.

There, she found a hut to live in and settled down.

Then, one evening there was a celebration. All the people were dancing and drinking corn beer, and the young man went to the hut where the young woman lived, and he asked her. "Why are you not dancing?"

Now, the young woman did not respond.

Then, the young man returned to the celebration, but he could not stop thinking about the young woman, and he returned.

There, he told her. "You are so beautiful. Would you be my woman?" And she replied. "I once had a man, but he forgot about me. I helped him, but he abandoned me. Why should I ever want to be married?" And the young man replied. "I would never be like the man that treated you badly."

Here, the messenger bird appeared and screamed at him. "Can you not see that this is your woman?"

Now, the man recognized his woman, and he declared. "You are my woman. Come with me." The young woman firmly replied. "I could never live with you as you are. You must become like me." And the young man replied. "I'll do whatever you want."

Then, the messenger bird fluttered violently, and the young man and woman were transformed into beautiful torcaces birds, and they flew out into the tall trees and never returned.

There, they live, and they are friendly to us, for they were once human.

Canto LXI

The Ant bear and the Jaguar

Tesere 12/27/1964

Now one day, an ant bear was sitting underneath a tree, and a jaguar came by and asked him. "What are you doing?" The ant bear replied. "I'm playing with my eyes. I take out one of my eyes, and later I take out the other, and I toss them up unto the tree and climb up the tree to find them, and I put them back in my head and do it over again." And the jaguar replied. "That looks like fun! Could I learn to play that game?" The ant bear replied. "Of course, you can."

Then, the jaguar tried to take out his eyes, but his paws were too big, and the jaguar exclaimed. "My paw is too big, for my eyes are so small. Can you help me?" The ant bear replied. "Yes, I can help you."

And so, the ant bear took out one of the jaguar's eyes and tossed it up the tree.

Then, the ant bear climbed up the tree and recovered the eye and returned the eye to the jaguar and placed it in his head.

Then, the ant bear asked the jaguar. "Did you enjoy that?" The jaguar replied. "Yes. I enjoyed it very much.

Now, take out both my eyes."

Then, the ant bear took out both of the jaguar's eyes and tossed them up the tree.

There, they remained.

Now, the jaguar was blind, and he called out. "Get my eyes from up out of that tree!" The ant bear replied. "Go get them yourself." And the jaguar exclaimed. "Can't you see that I'm blind!" The ant bear replied. "Yes! I can see that you are an idiot."

Then, the ant bear laughed, and the jaguar roared. "Give me my eyes!" And the ant bear smiled.

Then, the ant bear abandoned the jaguar, and after two days in the hot sun the jaguar's eyes began to decompose, and vultures appeared. The jaguar pleaded with the vultures. "Dear brothers don't eat my eyes, for the ant bear has played a cruel trick upon me. If you return my eyes to me, I will hunt again, and once again you will feast upon the remains of the kill."

Here, the vultures listened to the pleas of the jaguar, and they returned his eyes to him, and they helped him put his eyes back in his head, but the jaguar's eyes had begun to decompose, and he could not see clearly during the day.

So now, jaguars hunt at night.

Then, he found the ant bear sleeping, and he killed her.

Now, the baby ant bear had been out looking for ants.

When he returned, he saw that the jaguar had killed his mother.

There, the jaguar said to him. "I've killed your mother because she wanted to kill me." And the baby jaguar responded. "I'm still very small. How can I live without her? My mother carried me on her back. You must carry me on your back."

Then, the little ant bear jumped upon the back of the jaguar and hugged it neck. The powerful front legs and claws of the ant bear broke the jaguar's neck.

And so, the baby ant bear revenged the death of his mother.

Now, ant bears are always fighting, and the jaguar always loses.

Canto LXII

The dog and the jaguar

Tesere 1/13/1964

And so, it came to pass that a jaguar and a dog were traveling together through the wilderness.

And there, the dog said to the jaguar. "You are much stronger than me, but I'm more intelligent than you." The jaguar said nothing.

Sometime later, the jaguar the dog met again. And the jaguar said to the dog. "They tell me that you can sing very well. Would you sing something for me?"

Now, the dog very proud of his voice, and he began to sing. And the jaguar responded. "Your voice is magnificent can you sing louder?"

Then, the dog opened his mouth so wide that he torn open the skin at the corners of his mouth.

Then, the dog could only say. "Yowl, Yowl, Yowl."

Now, the jaguar felt sorry for the dog and said to him. "Come over here, and I will help you."

And so, the dog went over, and the jaguar took a spine and a thread of totai fiber and sewed up the corners over the dog's mouth.

Then, the dog was able to speak again.

Later, the jaguar and the dog met in the tall trees, and the jaguar asked him. "Has your mouth healed? Can you sing again?" The dog felt very flattered and began to sing.

Then, he opened his mouth all the way and broke open the wounds, but this time the jaguar did not help him.

Now, the dog can only Yowl.

Now, dogs hate jaguars, and when they chase jaguars, they always stay behind until the jaguar loses.

Now, you can see where the stiches of the jaguar's sewing were torn out, for the lips of a dog's mouth cross over at the corners of their mouths.

Canto LXIII

The Arapapa birds

Tesere 12/3/1964

One day a hunter went alone into the tall trees. As we all know hunting alone is foolish.

When he did not return after nightfall, his friend went out to look for him.

There, he called and called his friend's name.

Then, his friend called and called back to him.

Here, they walked towards the sound of each other's voice, yet they could never find each other. Soon both hunters were hopelessly lost.

And so, they never returned to their village, but they never gave up looking for each other.

Now, they are arapapa birds, and you can them calling to each other. Their song is very sad, for they can never find each other.

Canto LXIV

The Chuubi bird

Tesere 1/26/1965

In the time before our time, when the animals were human, there lived a man and his wife. They were happy together, but the man' brother hated his sister-in-law.

Then one day, the man's brother asked his sister-in-law law. "Would you need to go out into the tall trees for something?" She replied. "Yes, I need some firewood."

And so, they went out into the tall trees.

There, the brother took a club and smashed his sister-in-law's head.

Then, he built a fire and put her body into it. He left her body in the fire until it was nothing but ashes.

When the brother returned to the village, his brother asked him. "Do you know where my wife is?" And the murderer replied. "We went out into the tall trees together. She was gathering firewood, and I was looking for honey. I just went a little way away from her, but I lost sight of her, so I returned to the place where we separated and waited for her, but she did not return. I waited there for her several hours, but there was no sign of her, so I returned. Don't worry, I'm sure that she will return soon."

Now, the woman did not return, and her husband went out to look for her. He searched everywhere, but he saw no sign of her.

Then, he looked down.

There, he saw her ashes in a fire pit and he realized what had happened.

Here, he no longer wished to return to his village. He changed himself into chuubi bird and started to sing, and he is still singing his sad song.

Now, you can hear him and remember why he is so sad.

Canto LXV

The Caiman and the monkey

Tesere 2/22/1965

Once upon a time, there was a monkey who lived alone on an island out in the lakes and swamps.

After a time, he grew bored, and wanted to leave the island.

Then one day, he said to himself. "I wish that I had a canoe, for it is time that I get out of here, so I can be with other monkeys and have a family." And when a caiman swam by, the monkey called out. "Friend caiman do you know of someone who might lend me a canoe? I want to get out of here." And the caiman replied. "Yes, I do, for I'm a canoe! Come and sit down on my back."

Now, the monkey was very much afraid of the caiman, but he was desperate to leave, so he climbed up upon the caiman's back, and they began their journey through a maze of endless rivers and lagoons.

Then, the monkey became bored and started to bother the caiman. He put his hands over the caiman's eyes, and the caiman couldn't see, and he thought it was funny. The caiman snapped at the monkey and protested. "Don't be so silly, I'll lose my way."

Then, the monkey stopped, but he began insulting the caiman. "You are a scaly old fart, how scabby you are, your skin is disgusting and revolting to look at!"

Now, the caiman grew very angry and hissed. "I'll swallow you, if you say anything more!" The caiman was ready to throw the monkey in the water, but the monkey cried. "I was only joking."

Now, the monkey was afraid of the caiman, and when they passed near a tree branch, the monkey with his long arms grabbed the branch and swung himself up into the tree.

Here, he felt safe, and he began to scream insults at the caiman. "Monster, scabby, fart, asshole you are hideous and foul smelling."

Then, the caiman jumped out of the water and tried to bite the monkey, but he could not reach him.

There, the monkey began to swing through the trees.

Then, the caiman left the water and pursued the monkey on land, but the monkey easily escaped, and he laughed at the caiman from the tops of the trees.

Then, the caiman gave up and returned to the water.

There, he called to the vultures. "Friends I will give you the body of a monkey if you help me." The vultures replied. "What do you want from us?" And the caiman said. "Fly to where the monkey is and tell him that his uncle the caiman is dead."

And so, the vultures went to where the monkey was and told him. "Your uncle the caiman is dead."

And so, the monkey went to examine the caiman.

There, he sat up in a tree and observed the caiman, and he saw the caiman's tail move, and the monkey screamed. "It was all a lie; you are still alive!" The caiman didn't answer.

Then, the monkey took three rocks, and each time the caiman snapped at him he threw a rock into the caiman's mouth and the caiman swallowed all of them.

Then, the monkey said. "You are a stupid rotten animal. You wanted to kill me!"

Then, the monkey went away, and the caiman became sick and died, and the vultures began to devour his carcass. When the monkey returned, he asked the vultures. "What are you doing here?" And the vultures replied. "We are eating the carcass of our brother caiman who you killed by throwing rocks in his mouth."

Now, the monkey was very sad, for he had only wanted to play a joke, and he had killed the caiman.

Caimans don't understand jokes, but the monkey didn't know.

Canto LXVI

The tortoise and the macaw.

Tesere 1/29/1965

In the time before our time, when all the animals lived together in peace, blue macaw woman and tortoise man were a pair, and they lived together in a village.

Then one day, while they were in the tall trees. Blue macaw woman said to tortoise man. "Climb up that cusi palm tree and throw down the fruit, for I would like to eat some cusi fruit."

And so, tortoise man went over to the cusi tree and tried to climb it. Although he made attempts to climb the cusi tree, he was unable to climb it.

Then, blue macaw woman flew over to the tree sat down by the fruit and ate.

There, tortoise man sat below waiting for his woman.

When blue macaw woman finished eating, she did not return to her husband. She flew away with her relations.

Then, she forgot about tortoise man, and when her relations reminded her about her husband, she replied. "Why would I want a man who can't even climb a tree and get me fruit?"

There, under the tree the tortoise sat waiting.

Then, he realized that his wife would not return, so he returned to their home and began to sing sad songs. His songs were very beautiful, and all the animal people admired them.

Then one day, blue macaw woman heard the beautiful sad songs of tortoise man, and she asked. "Who is that who is singing over there?" And they replied. "It is your husband tortoise man." And blue macaw woman was very surprised and she exclaimed. "My husband! I never knew that he could sing so beautifully."

Then, blue macaw woman flew to the house of her husband and declared. "I did not know that you could sing such beautiful songs. I want to live with you again." The tortoise man did not respond, yet he continued to sing. Once again, blue macaw woman said. "I want to live with you again."

Then, tortoise man replied. "You abandoned me, and what was can never be again."

Now, blue macaw woman was very sad, for it was true.

Canto LXVII

The tick and the heron

Hapik'wa 2/5/1965

And so, it came to pass that one day a tick and a heron were talking. And the tick said to the heron. "Brother would you like to make a bet with me?" And the heron replied. "Yes, I would, but what do you have to wager?" And the tick replied. "We could have a race, and the one who gets to that tree over there is the winner. If I lose, you can kill me, and if you lose, I can sit on your back and drink your blood."

Then, the heron and the tick agreed.

Then, they met at the starting line.

Then, the heron began running, and the tick jumped on the heron's foot.

The heron ran faster and faster, but the tick held on, and right before the finish line the tick leaped forward and crossed the line ahead of the tick.

Now, the tick had won the race, and ticks attach themselves to animals and drink their blood.

Canto LXVIII

The cricket and the bee

Tesere 2/4/1965

In that time, when the animals were still taking between each other, the bee said to the cricket. "Within a short time, the cold south wind will blow, and you will have nothing to eat, so what will you do then?" And the cricket replied. "I don't know." And the bee said. "Come let us work together, so that we will be prepared for the cold south wind." And the cricket exclaimed. "No, I don't want to work. I'm too busy exploring. The world is lovely to fly about. There are beautiful wetlands, tall green trees, and flowers full of honey. I don't want to work; I want to laugh and sing." And the bee replied. "DO want you want."

Then, the bee flew away, and the cricket flew over to a flower.

There, he made lovely music by fiddling with his wings.

Then, cold south wind began to blow, and the cricket had nothing to eat, and the bee returned and spoke. "Now, do you understand, for you have nothing to eat." And the cricket replied. "Would you give me something to eat, for I'm very hungry." And the ant replied. "I'm not going to give you anything. It would be better if you were dead, for lazy animals like you are worthless."

Then, the bee flew away, and the cricket cried of hunger. The cricket knew that he would soon die.

Then, a great ant appeared and asked the cricket. "Why are you crying?" And the cricket replied. "I have nothing to eat, and I'm going to die." And the ant replied. "Come with me, for I have plenty of manioc in my garden."

Now, the ant was a good gardener, and he had planted rich fields.

And so, the cricket went to live to live with the great ant.

There, he lives today, and he does not go out into the cold southern wind.

Canto LXIX

How an ant helped a man

Tarekuve 2/14/1965

And so, it came to pass that there was a man who possessed a very deep well.

His well was the deepest in the entire village, and he was very proud of his well, and he would sing. "I have the most beautiful well. My well is the deepest of all."

Now, there were two friends who lived in this village, and one day they talked about the proud man and his well. "Let's go over and look at that well." And his friend replied. "We had better not, for that proud man might throw us into that well." His friend insisted. "It would be alright."

And so, the two friends went over to the well.

There, they saw the proud man and heard him singing. "I have the most beautiful well. My well is the deepest of all."

Then, the proud man called out to the two friends. "Come over here, and we will dance and celebrate my beautiful well." One of the friends replied. "No, I don't want to dance and celebrate." The other friend replied. "We must dance and celebrate."

And so, the proud man and the two friends began to celebrate and dance around the well.

Then, the proud man pushed one of them into the well.

Then, the other friend ran away, and the proud man chased him and tried to throw him in the well too.

Now, the friend who was deep in the well cried out. "Help me! Help me out of this well." The proud man laughed and replied. "Go and die down there."

He did not know what to do, and he cried. "Help me! Help me please! I'm trapped in this well."

Then, he thought. "I'll call to the animals to help me." He called to the mouse, but the mouse said. "I cannot help you." He called to the snake, but the snake could not help him. He called to the worm, the flea, the rat, and the bat, but none of them could help, and all of them waited for him to die.

Then came a tiny red ant, and the ant said to him. "I will help you brother. Just climb upon my back."

And so, the man climbed upon the back of the tiny ant, and the ant brought him out of the hole.

Canto LXX

The stupidity of the jaguar

Tesere 2/24/1965

Now, there was a group of men seated around a fire talking.

Nearby, a jaguar was hiding in the bushed waiting for a chance to attack.

Here, one of the men spoke. "What would you do if a jaguar attacked? I know what I would do. I would take my bow and arrow and kill it." Another man said. "I would take my knife and kill it and skin it." And another man said. "I would shoot it with my penis."

Then, all the men laughed.

The jaguar listened attentively, and he thought. "I know what bows and arrows are. I know what a knife is, but I don't know what kind of weapon a penis is."

Now, the jaguar was full of fear, and he decided not to attack, for he did not know how to prepare for the attack of a penis. The following day, the jaguar went to the river.

There, he saw a young woman.

Then, he leaped up in front of the woman, and he said to her. "If you tell me what kind of weapon a penis is, I will not kill you."

The woman lifted her skirt and opened her legs and spoke. "Do you see this blood." And the jaguar nodded. "Here is where a man wounded me with his penis, and this wound will never heal. Come and put your paw on this wound and then smell your paw."

And so, the jaguar put his paw on her vagina and exclaimed. "It is indeed rotten! The penis must be a horrible weapon."

Then, the jaguar left the menstruating woman go, for jaguars are very stupid.

Cantos influenced by Christianity

Canto LXXI

Jesus upon the earth

Tesere 2/28/1965

Once upon a time, Jesus and his servant Peter wandered over the earth. And it came to pass that in their travels they met a man.

Jesus drew near the man and spoke. "Give us something to eat." The man would give them nothing.

And so, Jesus turned the flesh of the man into worms.

Then, Jesus and Peter continued. They came upon another man and Jesus said to him. "Give us something to eat. The man gave them some feathers, and Jesus turned the feathers into chickens, and they cooked and ate the chickens.

And so, Jesus and Peter continued. They came to a place where a priest was saying mass, and Jesus asked him. "Where can we find water?" And the priest said to them impatiently. "Just go over there."

And so, Jesus and Peter went a long way in the direction the priest had waved, but they found no water.

Now, Jesus was very angry, and he returned and said to the priest. "I'm going to take your hair."

And from that time, priests have no hair on the top of their heads.

Once when the Jews were after Jesus, they asked Jesus's grandfather. "How can we find Jesus?" And the grandfather replied. "He is the one over there with a beard." And the Jews replied. "All of them have beards."

Then, the grandfather went over to Jesus and kissed him, and the Jews took him away. They put him in prison.

There, they planned to kill him, but Jesus escaped.

Then, he went to the sky.

Now, Jesus lives in the sky.

Canto LXXII

How the savages came into the world

Tesere 2/28/1965

It is not clear to which group Tesere is referring to, but the Siriono of eastern Bolivia were one of the most technologically limited people in the world. They could use and manufacture a few rudimentary tools, and they did not possess the skill to make fire and had to borrow it from there neighbors.

In the time long passed, Adam lived alone.

Everywhere, he walked alone.

Then one day, he saw a macaw copulating with his female, an Adam wanted to have a woman. He asked God. "Would you make a woman for me?" And God replied. "I'll make a woman for you, but you must never copulate with her."

And so, God made Adam a woman and gave her to him.

Then, the devil came to Adam and spoke. "You need to copulate with that woman. If you don't copulate with her, you cannot make babies. Go ahead and do it."

Then, Adam copulated with his woman.

Now, God was watching, and when Adam had finished, God said to him. "You can no longer live in the tall trees, and you must plant and plow the earth. You must baptize your children, and never make more children than you can handle."

Adam made many so children that he felt ashamed, so he hid a boy and a girl out in the tall trees. And when God came to baptize his children, Adam lied to God about the boy and girl hiding out in the tall trees.

After God had baptized all the children that Adam brought him, he said to Adam. "You have lied to me, for you still have a boy and a girl out in the tall trees. From now on they will live in the wilderness."

There, the wild people live in darkness.

Now, all Christians baptize their children, and the boy and girl left out in the tall trees are the progenitors of the savage people.

Canto LXXIII

Why the tortoise carries his house upon his back

Tesere 2/28/1965

God and Mary were lovers, and he made her pregnant.

And when it was time for her to give birth, he constructed a house of palm branches for her to live in.

Then, a child was born, and they called him Jesus. And their donkey proclaimed. "Jesus our savior is born. Oh, come let us adore him."

Then, the tapir said to the tortoise. "Come with me, and we will admire the baby Jesus." And the tortoise replied. "No, I wish to remain here and build a house."

Then, Jesus grew angry an made a house grow on the tortoise's back.

Now, the tortoise must carry his home upon his back, for he failed to admire the baby Jesus. Jesus is a powerful man but not as powerful as our grandfather Yaneramai.

Canto LXXIV

The origin of sand fleas and mosquitos.

Tesere 2/29/1965

Jesus's servant Paul was a good fisherman, and he was always sent out for fish.

Then, he would return and grill all the fish he had caught.

Then one time, he stayed out the whole night.

And when he returned, he fell asleep while he was grilling his catch, and all the fish burned to ashes.

Then, Paul went to Jesus and spoke. "I fell asleep while I was grilling the fish, and they all burned to ashes." And Jesus replied. "Go out tonight and fish again, but take this horn with you and blow on it when you feel sleepy."

And so, Paul went out to fish.

And when he felt sleepy, he blew into the horn, and many mosquitos flew out. They poked Paul, but he still fell asleep, and he did not fish that night.

Then next morning, Paul said to Jesus. "I went fishing, but I could not stay awake, and those mosquitos in the horn did not help."

And so, Jesus said to Paul. "Take this horn with you, and when you feel sleepy blow into it."

And so, Paul took the horn with him, and when he felt sleepy, he blew into the horn, and a host of sand fleas flew out of the horn, and they poked Paul.

This time, Paul did not sleep.

Now, there are mosquitos and sand fleas in the world.

Cantos of the recent past

Canto LXXV

The true story of the wanderings and settlements of the Guarasug'we

Tesere 2/28/1965

This is an oral history of the Guarasug'we. It is unlike all the other Cantos contained in this book, for it is not literature. It is an attempt by Tesere to give a realistic account of the final days of the Guarasug'we. The poetic form does apply here as a historical rhetorical device.

Now, I have nothing more to tell you, for you already know everything about us. I've told you our entire history. I would not have told you these stories, if I thought that you would not take them seriously. These stories were of the village of Guarasug'we who lived on the banks of the Paraqua' river.

Additionally, I would not have told you these stories, if they were not revealed in dreams.

In a little while, my serata soul will depart, and it will find the soul of my deceased brother the shaman Awa'a. And as he said to me. "So, as the tree will die, so will come the end. They are in fear of the end, and soon everything will end."

Quickly, we shall come to the end, so, therefore, I've told you our sacred stories, and I can see that you (Dr. Riester) have carefully recorded them, for you are able to read them back to me. I will not say anything more of our certain end.

However, I don't want you to finish before recording this last part. This last part is sad, and it is not playful like the stories that you already know. I will give you an accurate account of our past.

Once the Guarasug'we were a much larger family. For many years there were two villages of Guarasug'we. One village lived on the banks of the Paraqua' river, and another village lived on the other bank of the Guapore River.

And before our division into two groups, we all lived happily together in a very large village on the banks of the Pauserna river. In those days there were no white people like there are now.

Our neighbors the Chiquitanos call us Pauserna. We do not like this name, for it means that we are savages. The name Guarasug'we is our hereditary name, and not the false name used for us by the Chiquitanos. My father and the old people of the tribe have told us that the name Pauserna our neighbors use for us comes from our practice of setting large wood posts into the ground to memorialize our ancestors. These posts helped us to remember the dead and missing.

After the Brazilians came to our village along the Pauserna river, they brought to us a terrible influenza and fever. We had never before experienced sickness as these. The Guarasug'we fled their villages along the Pauserna river. Once there had been ten large villages of Guarasug'we and each village had a chief and two sub chiefs.

We all abandoned our villages along the Pauserna river, some of the Guarasug'we went to the Guapore River, and some of them went to the Paraqua' river. Still others left the area completely. There was a great quantity of displaced people, as all the Guarasug'we left their villages along the Pauserna river. It was a time of great suffering, and many died, and many others were lost. Once, they had lived happily along the Pauserna river, but all that came to an end.

However, our history was not over. A group of Guarasug'we settled along the banks of the Paraqua river. It was there that I was born. When I was still a small child, the rubber boom came to our village, and the workers caused us a great deal of suffering.

The old people talk of how we were once a great tribe with many children before we abandoned our villages on the Pauserna and relocated to the Guapore River. We came to a place where the steam Bella Vista empties into a lagoon, and there many more died of fever. They simply dropped dead while they were drinking water and talking with their friends.

The sister of my mother got out of bed one morning and went to get some water and never returned. All of our people went out to look for her, and they found the poor thing near the water source. Blood was coming out of her mouth, y she was feverish and could barely speak, but she managed to say. "This fever comes from the white people. We are all going to die if we don't get out of here quickly." Many more people died so many more.

I am the son of Kunumis. My mother is called Pesu. Savui is my brother and Hapik'wa my sister. My father was the chief. The current chief is Tarecure. On the other side of the river was the chief Ovopyte.

When both villages of Guarasug'we lived on the banks of the Pauserna river, we were not at war. After our people separated, the ones who lived along the Guapore River and those who lived along the Paraqua river began fighting with each other. Those people along the Guapore River were warlike, and sometimes we fought back with courage and valor. They would attack us and try to take our women, but we fought them and drove them away.

My father told me that the Guarasug'we along the Guapore River were hit hard by influenza. Their losses were much greater than ours, and many more of them died. And after their chief Fortunado died, there were very few of them left. My woman Yeruv'sa is of the Guapore River people, and so is Tariku. All of the clan along the Guapore River came over to us after the death of their chief Ovopyte.

At the present time, we are all living here together as we once did along the Pauserna river. Now, there are so few of us. My mother Pesu told me about our ancestors, and how they not only lived along the Pauserna river. Before our time along the Pauserna river, we lived in the area around the city of San Ignacio.

Long ago our people traveled long distances. They were not like we are now, for we have become idle and tired. Back then, they would travel a little and then stop to rest. They traveled in a secession of short distances repeatedly until they came to where they stopped and settled down. Before, our people were brave and intrepid travelers who would only settle down for short times, and they would relentlessly search for new ground.

In the old days, the Guarasug'we were led by a shaman. It was a shaman who led us to the area near where the city of San Ignacio is now located. There, our people lived for many generations. The ancestors of my mother told her the story of how our ancestors, and the ancestors of our ancestors lived. They are the ones who told her our history. Our history near the area where now sets the city of San Ignacio before we lived along the Paragu'a river and the Guapore River. Before we all lived together along the Pauserna river. All this happened a long time ago, and as I've already told you; our ancestors knew the story.

When my father Kunumis was not very old, the white men came. They came to our villages, and all the Guarasug'we fled into the tall trees. There, they stayed for a long time. After they abandoned our villages, we found axes, knives, steel machetes, cotton clothes, hair combs and many other things. And when our people came back out of hiding, they were delighted to find and use all the things that the white men had left behind.

Our people liked the steel tools, and that is how we lost or way. And when the white men returned, most of our people did not flee into the tall trees. Only a few women and children and a few men fled into the tall trees. The majority of our people remained in our village with the white men. The white men put many pretty things in a great house, and many of our people went inside. There, they were surrounded, and they were shot if they tried to escape, and many were mortally wounded.

Those men and women who were trapped inside the great house were taken away. Those Guarasug'we who had not entered the house filled with pretty things remained in the tall trees until the white men left.

The white men marched those they had captured to the city of Santa Cruz de la Sierra. Santa Cruz in much farther away than San Ignacio.

In the city of Santa Cruz, the white men sold our people. Nearly all the children died on the way to Santa Cruz. The white men rapped the women, and they raped the young girls who were still virgins. The white men had no respect for women. They were cruel with us.

A few of our people returned from Santa Cruz and told us what had happened. They told us about the city and the road to the city. They desired to return to the city, for there were many things there. They returned to the city by crossing the land of the Guarayos. The Guarayos speak almost the language that we speak, but they speak it very oddly. They speak in a strange way, but we are able to understand each other.

In the land of the Guarayos, the white men sold our people like they sell rubber. Those who escaped from the slavers told us about how our people were taken to the Beni River.

It is because of all these things that our people do not like the white men, for they are wicked and evil people. The white men who slept with their own daughters every year would kill the children that they produced.

Yaneramai does not want us to live with the white people. We know this because our shaman has told us. Whenever the end of the world comes, we do not want to lose our souls. If the end comes soon, it will be terrible because there are so many people. The end will come, and the earth will be destroyed and all the people will die.

The end for all people is coming, and people will never return to earth. Our people are very few, and the end of our people is coming soon. Before the end, we have to get free and separate ourselves from the white men, for they are without souls, and they can never be saved.

However, there was a white man with a soul. He was not Brazilian, Bolivian, or Chiquitano. He told us his name was Father Enrique. He spoke our language, Portuguese, Spanish, and another language. He taught us some word of his language. In his language the word for water was vaser, and in his language the word for tree was baum. Our chief could understand Father Enrique when he spoke our language.

Father Enrique was our father, and he was very good to us. He bought our rubber, our animal skins and paid us a very good and fair price. He was not a cheat like other white men. He was always friendly to everyone. He was a very good minister to us.

At the time he died, we were located in Suviuhu. Other white men arrived and wanted us to slash the rubber trees collect the sap and sell it to them. Other white men arrived and wanted us to collect the rubber tree sap and sell it to them. We did not like to work as the Chiquitanos worked. We could sell our rubber, poalla, and skins for a better price to the traders on the Guapore River.

Mister Jurgen Riester is our friend, like father Enrique. We hope that Mister Riester will always be with us, but we know that someday he will go. Our end is coming soon no more than two to thirteen years. I believe that our young people know that our time as a people is over, and they have no interest in the stories of our ancestors.

Canto LXXVI

The death of Kunumis

Hapik'wa 12/1/1964

My father was a good man.

And when he was ready to die, he called us all before him and said this:

My children I'm going to leave you. Last night your grandfather's ghost came to visit me. He had been brought to the from house of the dead by Yancrataque. And together we returned to the house of the dead.

There, I saw many animals of the wilderness and great fields of manioc and corn. I saw many people working out in those fields, and they all looked very happy to be working. I felt thirsty, and I asked my father for some water, and he replied. "Not yet, first we must return to the earth and say good bye. Then when you return, we can drink, and we will have a grand celebration. All the people will paint their faces orange, and we will dance."

So, spoke my father Kunumis, as he laid in his hammock, and we were gathered around him.

Then, he told us:

Don't be sad, for I've returned here once more to tell you not to cry and not to grieve for more than a day. Soon they will come for me. Everyone here on earth will someday die, but where I'm going, now, there is no death.

Then, Kunumis settled comfortably into his hammock, and his spirit left and went to the Serata Sea. Awa'a our shaman put his hands over the head of Kunumis and announced that our father had left for Serata.

Then, we cried for only a day as he had told us to do.

Now, I think of my father. He will be filled with joy when he sees me crossing over. He will stand by the river and to welcome me across. Our family will be reunited, and I wait with anticipation for that happy day. I will no longer grieve for more than a day, for I know that we will all be together again.

Canto LXXVII

Hapik'wa's dream

Hapik'wa 11/15/1964

Once when I was sick, I saw me deceased brother Awa'a. He had been a shaman when he was alive. He covered my body with the orange paint of the urucu bush, and decorated my body with his prettiest feathers.

Then, the ghost of my brother said to me. "Sister you are sick. Do you want to go to the house of the dead?" And I told him. "I don't want to go, for I have a grandson to care for." And he replied. "You must take the medicine that I give you."

Then, he gave me good medicine, and I continued to live on the earth and care for my grandson. I wasn't ready to leave with my brother until my grandson was grown, for that was my duty. I knew that he would return when my grandson no longer needed me.

Now, I know that my bother will someday return for me, and we will travel together through the fields of manioc and urucu.

There, we will travel in a procession of other souls though the hole in the sky and arrive at the house of the dead.

There, we will drink and be merry, and we will never grow old and die.

Canto LXXVIII

Hapik'wa's Dream

Hapik'wa 1/18/1965

Last night a toad came to see me. It was a terrible toad. It had large eyes end enormous feet. I was very much afraid of this giant toad.

Then, the ghost of my father appeared, and I went into the sky with him. We went to heaven. How beautiful it was there! All the people were dressed in feathers and painted orange.

There, I saw many people.

Then, the giant sky worm wanted to kill me, and I began to cry. The ghost of my father said to me. "Do not cry, since I'm with you the sky worm will not be able to harm you."

Next, I spoke with many members of my family. They gave me many delicious foods, and we began to celebrate. I wanted to speak with Ya-neramai, but they told me not to. "Yaneramai will not let you speak to him. He will speak to you after your death. Now, he only speaks with powerful shamans."

Here, I'm already old, and I no longer desire to live on earth. I'm tired, and I want to return to heaven and see my family.

I want to be with them forever. There in the house of the dead. It is very beautiful.

Now, I'm old and soon the ghost of my father will come to carry me home.

Works Cited

Bierhorst, John. 2002. *The Mythology of South America*. Oxford, England: Oxford University Press.

Levi-Strauss. 1967. *Structural Anthropology*. Garden City, New York: Anchor Books.

Lewis, Oscar. 1963. *The Children of Sanchez*. New York: Vintage Books.

Metraux, Alfred. 1942. The Native Tribes of Eastern Bolivia and Western Matto Grosso.

Nickol, Robert. 1994. *Native American Discourse*. Missoula, Montana: unpublished thesis University of Montana.

Reed, Richard. 1995. *Prophets of Agroforestry*. Austin: University of Texas.

Riester, Jurgen. 1977. *Los Guarasug'we Cronica de sus Ultimos Dias*. La Paz: Los Amigos del libro.

Service, Elman. 1954. *Spanish Guarani Relations in early Colonial Paraguay*. Ann Arbor, Michigan: Anthropological Papers no. 9.

Steward, Julian. 1959. *Native Peoples of South America*. York, Pennsylvania: Maple press.